THE CATCH-UP GUIDE TO
DOCTOR WHO

Other Works by Valerie Estelle Frankel

Henry Potty and the Pet Rock: An Unauthorized Harry Potter Parody

Henry Potty and the Deathly Paper Shortage

Buffy and the Heroine's Journey

From Girl to Goddess: The Heroine's Journey in Myth and Legend

Katniss the Cattail: An Unauthorized Guide to Names and Symbols in The Hunger Games

The Many Faces of Katniss Everdeen: Exploring the Heroine of The Hunger Games

Harry Potter, Still Recruiting: An Inner Look at Fandom

An Unexpected Parody: The Unauthorized Spoof of The Hobbit Movie

Teaching with Harry Potter

Myths and Motifs in The Mortal Instruments

Winning the Game of Thrones: The Host of Characters and their Agendas

Winter is Coming: Symbols, Portents, and Hidden Meanings in A Game of Thrones

Bloodsuckers on the Bayou: The Myths, Symbols, and Tales Behind HBO's True Blood

The Girl's Guide to the Heroine's Journey

Doctor Who and the Hero's Journey

Doctor Who - The What, Where, and How: A Fannish Guide to the TARDIS-Sized Pop Culture Jam

Choosing to Be Insurgent or Allegiant: Symbols, Themes, and Analysis of the Divergent Trilogy

Sherlock: Every Canon Reference You May've Missed in BBC's Series 1-3

Women in Game of Thrones

Symbols in Game of Thrones

How Game of Thrones Will End

Joss Whedon's Names

Pop Culture in the Whedonverse

THE CATCH-UP GUIDE TO
DOCTOR
WHO

Repeat Characters, Plot Arcs, Heroes, Monsters, and the Doctor All Made Clear

Valerie Estelle Frankel

The season arc guides and Whoniverse Episode Guide are adapted from *Doctor Who - The What, Where, and How: A Fannish Guide to the TARDIS-Sized Pop Culture Jam,* while the history of River Song comes from *Doctor Who and the Hero's Journey* and the review of *Adventures in Space and Time* was previously posted on valeriefrankel.wordpress.com.

The Catch-Up Guide to Doctor Who is an unauthorized guide and commentary on *Doctor Who* (show and related media) and its related universe. None of the individuals or companies associated with the books or television series or any merchandise based on this series have in any way sponsored, approved, endorsed, or authorized this book.

Contents

9

Introduction

Everyone loves *Doctor Who* – the Police Box, sonic screwdriver, timey-wimey gadgets, cool bowties and fezzes, suits, trainers, and endless running. There's companions in miniskirts and sexy time travelers River Song and Captain Jack. Still with fifty-one years of episodes (including countless novels, audio adventures, minisodes, extras, and more), it's hard to know where to start. Will watching "Rose" cover everything needed? Who are the monsters dragged from the older episodes? What about the complex time travel arcs lasting three years or more? How many hundreds of in-jokes are there, and could someone explain them? In this book, all is made clear, from plot arcs to key items, characters, and species. Who is the Doctor and what do we know about him? Where are he and his companions heading as the reboot approaches its tenth year? From TARDIS Cloister Bell to 3D glasses, jelly babies to invasions of London, let's find out.

Creating the Show

Doctor Who was created by Sydney Newman, who also created the popular British show *The Avengers*. As Head of Drama at BBC, he asked Verity Lambert to produce a time travel children's program. As the Doctor visited different times, a young student in tow, it would be educational. Episodes were a half-hour each, in multi-part serials (often four parts, but sometimes as many as ten or as few as one). The Doctor himself is established as a mystery down to his name, his race, and whether he was a criminal fleeing his home planet. The police box was chosen as time machine because they were so ubiquitous at the time. This was also a budget saver, as a simple wooden box that disappeared and reappeared without actually flying. Meanwhile, the theme music, designed by Ron Grainer aided by Delia Derbyshire, has remained unchanged for half a century.

Sydney Newman ruled that there were to be "no bug-eyed monsters," but Verity Lambert liked Terry Nation's Dalek script and made it the second episode. Children adored the creatures, and the Daleks became the show's most iconic villains. This historical episodes continued for a time, intermingled with science fiction stories. However, after the Second Doctor serial *The Highlanders,* only one other pure historical appeared. The bug-eyed aliens stole the show.

Popular producers that followed include Barry Letts (1970-1975) and Nathan Turner (1980-1989). In the Fourth Doctor era, producer Graham Williams (1977-1980) worked with scriptwriters Robert Holmes, Anthony Read, and

Douglas Adams, all of whom wrote some of the show's most beloved scripts. The James-Bond-style Third Doctor (Jon Pertwee) and especially the quirky Fourth Doctor (Tom Baker) brought the show many new fans.

The show lasted through seven Doctors and a host of companions and was finally canceled in 1989. An American TV movie offered a handsome Eighth Doctor in Paul McGann, the first to show romantic feelings toward his companion, but the movie did not lead to a rebooted series as hoped.

In 2005, Russell T Davies rebooted the show with Christopher Eccleston as Ninth Doctor and companion Rose Tyler, played by pop star Billie Piper. This was a quick success, and the Doctor who followed, David Tennant raised the popularity to unheard-of levels. As the David Tennant era ended in 2009, Davies handed the show over to Steven Moffat, whose episodes such as "The Empty Child" and "Blink" had impressed viewers with their spookiness and power. His Doctor, Matt Smith, continued to raise devotion to the program, and he and David Tennant joined for the Fiftieth Anniversary special in 2013. His Doctor regenerated in the Christmas special that followed into number Twelve, Peter Capaldi.

About The Doctor

Childhood

Very little has been seen of the Doctor's youth on the planet Gallifrey. Susan describes the planet saying, "The sky is a burnt orange and the leaves of the trees are silver" (*The Sensorites*). The Tenth Doctor says almost the same sentence in "Gridlock." A few defining moments have appeared: In "The Sound of Drums," the Doctor describes a Time Lord Academy initiation ceremony (seen in "The End of Time") where, at age eight, each Time Lord child is forced to gaze into the Untempered Schism, a gap in space and time where they can view the Time Vortex. Some are inspired, some go mad, and some run away. This madness overtook the Master, who heard the "sound of drums" thereafter. The Doctor, by contrast, notes he was one of "the ones that ran away; I never stopped!"

The Doctor's crib has been seen ("A Good Man Goes to War") and the Doctor describes various children's books like *Snow White and the Seven Keys to Doomsday* ("Night Terrors"). Young Gallifreyan children are sometimes called "Time Tots," as Romana later describes herself (*Shada*).

A childhood moment has also been seen with Clara comforting him in his room. For some of his childhood, the Doctor ostracized himself, going to sleep in a barn where he would weep over his fears. Clara Oswald comforted him in his distress, assuring him that fear gave him strength ("Listen"). When Madame de Pompadour read his mind, she said he was "such a lonely little boy" ("The Girl in the Fireplace").

Older, the Doctor attended the Academy alongside the Master, at the time his friend. He attended the Time Lord Academy under the tutelage of Borusa and was a member of the Prydonian Chapter (*The Deadly Assassin*). The Master was one of his classmates (*The Five Doctors*). The Doctor did not have an impressive career at school, passing his qualifying exams to become a Time Lord with only 51% – the lowest possible pass mark – on the second attempt (*The Ribos Operation*).

Eventually, he found a TARDIS waiting and "borrowed" it (it's unclear whether he ever meant to return it). With his granddaughter Susan and a series of human (and occasionally nonhuman) companions, he journeyed on many adventures.

Regeneration

> BEN: The Doctor always wore this. If you are him it should fit... That settles it!
> SECOND DOCTOR: I'd like to see a butterfly fit into a chrysalis case after it spreads its wings.
> POLLY: Then you *did* change."
> SECOND DOCTOR: Life depends on change, and renewal.
> BEN: Oh, that's it, you've been renewed, have you?"
> SECOND DOCTOR: Renewed? Have I? That's it, I've been renewed. It's part of the TARDIS. Without it I couldn't survive. (*The Power of the Daleks*)

In his final story, *War Games*, the Second Doctor notes that Time Lords can live forever, "barring accidents." However, when a Time Lord is critically injured, dying, or possibly dead, he can regenerate into a new body. In *The Deadly Assassin*, the Doctor says that Time Lords can only regenerate a total of twelve times. The Eleventh Doctor, when visiting *The Sarah Jane Adventures* for *Death of the Doctor*, flippantly states he can regenerate "507" times. This is most likely a joke or a code (five plus seven equals twelve). Several times even before "A Town Called Christmas," the limit on lives is implied to be a law of the Time Lord Council. In *The Five Doctors* the Time Lords offer the Master, a regeneration cycle as reward for his help and cooperation, and the regenerate him again to fight in the Time War. Neil Gaiman, author of many bestselling novels as well as episodes "The Doctor's Wife" and "Nightmare in Silver" explains:

> It's interesting, that rule. It was obviously bendable to begin with (the Time Lords gave the Master a whole new round of regenerations). So I've always thought that it was more a law like a speed limit is a law than like Gravity is a law. And if there are no longer any police to make you observe the speed limit, you can drive as fast as you like. Although it's a lot more dangerous. (Q & A: Neil Gaiman)

The War Doctor and the Tenth Doctor's aborted regeneration in "The Stolen Earth"/ "Journey's End" count among his regenerations, bringing him to his final incarnation in "The Time of the Doctor"…before the Time Lords send him an entirely new set. Nonetheless, the Twelfth Doctor claims he "won't keep regenerating forever" ("Kill the Moon").

The episode "The Doctor's Wife" establishes (through a brief remark about the Corsair) that Time Lords can switch gender during regeneration. This is later seen in "Dark Water." While many regenerations appear uncontrolled, the Doctor has a controlled regeneration into the War Doctor and Romana is seen to be choosing her face (fan theories on this range from her having more talent and/or better technology to the scene being a hologrammatic fake-out). *The Mark of the Rani* confirms that women can direct the process more than men – even Melody Pond in "Let's Kill Hitler" says she's focusing on a specific dress size. The head of the Sisterhood of Karn tells the Doctor, "our elixir can trigger your regeneration, bring you back. Time Lord science is elevated here on Karn. The change doesn't have to be random. Fat or thin, young or old, man or woman?"("Night of the Doctor").

The Doctor's Age

In the show, accounts vary. Two says he's roughly 450 years old, but later Doctors say they've traveled for 900 years ("The Empty Child") or 700 ("The Doctor's Wife"). He's 748 in *Planet of the Spiders*, 759 in *The Pirate Planet*, 953 by the Seventh Doctor's *Time and the Rani*. Nine says he's 900 years old. Over series six, the Eleventh Doctor ages from 909 to 1103, reaching age 1200 for his final Christmas special. Several possibilities appear, from the Gallifreyan vs. human year count and the possibility that the Doctor has forgotten or miscalculated.

The Doctor's Name

In the first episode, Barbara calls the Doctor "Doctor Foreman," as this is Susan's fake surname. When Ian echoes this, the Doctor responds, "Eh? Doctor who? What's he talking about?" Trying to figure this out, Ian asks Barbara, "Who is he? Doctor who?" An early note had Barbara and Ian actually calling him "Doctor Who" because they didn't know his name, while another had the Doctor wandering about with amnesia, with this catchphrase used because he couldn't recall his own name. While this idea was abandoned, he remained "Doctor Who" in the credits for decades. There was also an episode titled *Doctor Who and the Silurians* and episode five of *The Chase* is titled "The Death of Doctor Who."

The computer WOTAN in *The War Machines* calls him Doctor Who and the Third Doctor's car, "Bessie," has the license plate WHO 1. In *The Highlanders*, the Second Doctor calls himself "Doctor von Wer" (German for "Doctor Who"), and signs his name as "Dr. W" in *The Underwater Menace*. He calls himself "the Great Wizard Quiquaequod" in *The Dæmons;* 'Qui," "quae," and "quod" being the various gendered forms of the Latin for "who."

There's a recurring joke that when our hero introduces himself as "The Doctor" someone will say, "Doctor Who?" The Daleks chant this in "Asylum of the Daleks" after their

18

memories are wiped. Question marks on the Fourth through Seventh Doctors' clothes are meant to nod to this.

> DOCTOR: Do you remember me?
> CLARA: No. Should I? Who are you?
> DOCTOR: The Doctor. No? The Doctor?
> CLARA: Doctor who?
> DOCTOR: No, just the Doctor. Actually, sorry, could you start all that again?
> CLARA: Could I what?
> DOCTOR: Could you just ask me that question again?
> CLARA: Doctor who?
> DOCTOR: Okay, just once more.
> CLARA: Doctor who?
> DOCTOR: Ooo, yeah. Ooo. Do you know, I never realised how much I enjoy hearing that said out loud. Thank you.
> CLARA: Okay.(shuts the door on him.) ("The Bells of Saint John")

Meanwhile, his most common alias is John Smith, first invented by the companion Jaime. His former classmate Drax calls the Doctor Theta Sigma or "Thete" for short in *The Armageddon Factor*, as it's his school nickname from the Prydon Academy on Gallifrey.

The story arc running through the Eleventh Doctor's time describes the name as the oldest question in the universe, hidden in plain sight." It has indeed been waiting in the credits all this time. Even Madame de Pompadour reads the Doctor's mind and asks, "Doctor who? It's more than just a secret, isn't it?" The Doctor tells his name to River and she tells it to him to establish her credentials when he first meets her in the library. As he remarks, there's only one time je would tell someone his name.

Clara reads the Doctor's name in *A History of the Time War* and reacts, suggesting it has significance for her, though she soon forgets it ("Journey to the Centre of the TARDIS"). In "The Name of the Doctor," the Doctor's real name is revealed to be the password to the Doctor's tomb on the planet Trenzalore. Likewise, the Time Lords project this question across all of time and space through a crack in the skin of the universe as a type of password only the Doctor can answer. In "The Time of the Doctor," he realizes that if he says his name, they will come through and bring disaster, a similar revelation to the one in "The Name of the Doctor."

There is also the significance of the chosen title "The Doctor," which even the Time Lords call him. In "The Sound of Drums," the Master calls him sanctimonious for identifying himself as "the man who makes people better." He may actually be a medical doctor, as he describes early on that he's studied under Joseph Lister and Joseph Bell. The Fourth Doctor calls himself "a doctor of many things" (*Revenge of the Cybermen*). In "A Good Man Goes to War," written by Moffat like the Doctor's name arc, River Song tells that the Doctor's travels have influenced the etymology of the word "doctor," perverting its meaning on some worlds from "wise man" or "healer" to "great warrior." "The Day of the Doctor" describes the name as a promise of the sort of man he wants to be: "Never cruel or cowardly. Never giving up and never giving in."

The Doctor's Family

References to the Doctor's family are rare. His granddaughter is his first companion as they flee Gallifrey together. She chooses to wed a human and stay with him in earth's future. Susan's descendants appear in some of the expanded universe stories but her final fate is uncertain.

In "Smith and Jones," the Doctor references having a brother. This may be a nod to expanded media – Irving Braxiatel, a character in several novels beginning with *Theatre of War*, is the Doctor's biological older brother. He becomes a recurring character in the Big Finish spinoffs *Gallifrey* and *Bernice Summerfield*.

The Doctor most often hints at his children and grandchildren being dead, though he doesn't provide details. In "The Empty Child," Dr. Constantine says to him, "Before this war began, I was a father and a grandfather. Now I'm neither. But I'm still a doctor." The Ninth Doctor replies,

"Yeah. I know the feeling."

As far as wives, the Doctor likely married Susan's grandmother, a Time Lady, and later marries River Song – part human and part Time Lady. He marries Queen Elizabeth I ("The Day of the Doctor") and possibly Marilyn Monroe ("A Christmas Carol") as well.

In the 1996 television movie, the Eighth Doctor remarks that he is half-human on his mother's side (this may be a joke). In *The End of Time*, a mysterious individual, referred to only in the credits as "The Woman," appears unexpectedly to Wilfred Mott throughout both episodes. She is later revealed to be a dissident Time Lady, who opposed the Time Lord High Council's plan to escape the Time War. In *Doctor Who: The Writer's Tale – The Final Chapter*, Russell T Davies states that he created the character to be the Doctor's mother and this is what actress Claire Bloom was told when she was cast.

Time Lords

The first six years of the show explained little about the Time Lords, save that the Doctor was running from them. Their first appearance is terrifying, as they strip the Doctor of his companions and force him to regenerate – a virtual death sentence.

The Gallifreyans discovered the ability to control time thanks to two people: Omega, a "stellar engineer" who detonated a star as a source of power, and Rassilon, who learned to harness the power of a black hole. From these experiments, Omega got trapped in the anti-matter universe but Rassilon survived and founded Time Lord society. Madame Vastra also speculates in "A Good Man Goes to War" that exposure to the Time Vortex via the Schism allowed the Gallifreyan species to evolve into Time Lords. They ruled the galaxy for ten million years, with absolute power (*The Ultimate Foe*).

In the early days, the Time Lords meddled with younger races and even kidnapped other species to take part in gladiatorial games for their amusement (as seen in *The Five*

Doctors). They elevated the people of Minyos until they tore their own planet apart. At last, they reformed and vowed never to interfere with other races. The Doctor, however, rebelled against the decree, stole a time machine from a repair yard, and went traveling around the galaxy with his granddaughter Susan, interfering wherever he wished.

Several other Time Lords act similarly, hiding on earth or other planets and doing as they please. Others of Gallifrey appear to oppose the policy – the Celestial Intervention Agency, or C.I.A., actually sends the Doctor on missions to interfere as necessary.

In *The Deadly Assassin,* the Doctor visits Gallifrey where the Master frames him for assassinating the president, and the Doctor temporarily becomes president himself! Much of the culture is seen, from the rather showy and incompetent Chancellory Guards to the Castellan who leads investigations. The Doctor, like the Master and the Rani, belongs to the Prydonian Clan of Gallifrey, known for devious cunning. The Doctor battles the Master's henchman inside the Matrix, a network of past and present Time Lord minds that acts as an enormous database and future forecaster. The Doctor realizes the Master is actually seeking the ceremonial relics given to the President on induction, the Sash and Rod of Rassilon, keys to the Eye of Harmony. This is the heart of a black hole captured by ancient Time Lord Rassilon, source of Time Lord power and capable of restarting a regeneration cycle. The Doctor stops him at last.

Other Time Lords include those with imposing titles: The War Chief, The Monk, the Corsair, and possibly the Celestial Toymaker. Others have actual names, from Romanadvora-trelundar (certainly a mouthful) to Morbius, Flavia, Borusa, Spandrell, Goth, Runcible, K'anpo Rimpoche, and Time Lord Founder Lord Rassilon. There are also the Doctor's granddaughter Susan (almost certainly an earth alias) and the Tenth Doctor's clone Jenny (named by Donna Noble).

In another adventure, the Doctor and the Master must work together to defeat the Doctor's old mentor Borusa. At the end, the Doctor receives a shocking promotion:

> FLAVIA: Doctor, you have evaded your responsibilities for far too long. The disqualification of President Borusa leaves a gap at the very summit of the Time Lord hierarchy. There is only one who can take this place. Yet again, it is my duty and my pleasure to inform you that the full Council has exercised its emergency powers to appoint you to the position of President, to take office immediately.
> DOCTOR 5: Oh, no.
> FLAVIA: This is a summons no Time Lord dare refuse. To disobey the will of the High Council will attract the severest penalties.
> DOCTOR 5: Very well, Chancellor Flavia. You will return to Gallifrey immediately and summon the High Council. You have full deputy powers until I return. I shall travel in my TARDIS.
> ...[Back on the TARDIS]
> TEGAN: It'll soon be goodbye, then.
> DOCTOR 5: Will it?
> TURLOUGH: Well, you're off to Gallifrey to be President. I suppose your Time Lord subjects will find a TARDIS that really works and get us both home?
> DOCTOR 5: Who said anything about Gallifrey?
> TURLOUGH: You told Chancellor Flavia
> DOCTOR 5: I told her she had full deputy powers until I returned.
> TEGAN: You're not going back?
> DOCTOR 5: You know, sometimes, Tegan, you take my breath away.
> TURLOUGH: Er, won't the Time Lords be very angry?
> DOCTOR 5: Furious.
> TEGAN: You mean you're deliberately choosing to go on the run from your own people in a rackety old TARDIS?
> DOCTOR 5: Why not? After all, that's how it all started.
> (*The Five Doctors*)

A proposed backstory, explored in Platt's 1997 novel *Lungbarrow*, has the Doctor co-founding Time Lord society with Rassilon and Omega. The Time Lords can no longer reproduce, and they use biotechnological Looms to "weave" new Time Lords.

While Time Lords resemble humans, they have two

hearts, a "respiratory bypass system" that can allow them to go without air, an internal body temperature of 15–16 degrees Celsius (60 degrees Fahrenheit), and of course, the ability to regenerate. The Doctor mentions in *The Mind of Evil* that a tablet of aspirin could kill him, and he dies because of uninformed surgery in the television movie. In "Cold Blood," a bacterial decontamination nearly kills him. There is some resistance to radiation, though it's inconstant between seasons and producers. Several episodes see him descending into a self-induced coma in order to heal.

In "The Fires of Pompeii," the Doctor reveals that he can perceive "fixed points" and "points in flux" in the fabric of time. The Doctor has limited telepathy, as he can link with other version of himself (*The Five Doctors*), and share memories with others (in "The Big Bang" and "The Lodger," among others). Madame de Pompadour reverses the process and reads the Doctor's mind in turn, saying, "A door, once opened, may be stepped through in either direction."

When a Time Lord finally dies, his corpse must be destroyed directly. River says, "A Time Lord's body is a miracle. Even a dead one. There are whole empires out there who'd rip this world apart for just one cell. We can't leave him here. Or anywhere" ("The Impossible Astronaut"). In "The Name of the Doctor," his less corporeal body appears as an index of his timestream, which people can actually enter.

In *Trial of a Time Lord* "The Time Lords are exposed as villains. They have interfered and lied to cover their tracks. They have killed millions and changed the fate of a planet" (Muir 367). They've meddled to establish superiority and dominate other races. After they're exposed as hypocrites blaming the Doctor to cover their deceptions, they aren't seen again. When the Ninth Doctor reveals they've died, he mourns, but as he reveals later, he has remembered them the way he wants.

In *The Five Doctors*, Rassilon is a wise leader, automatically trapping those who covet immortality and eternal power. By the Tenth Doctor's time, however, he seems to have grown greedy and corrupt. The Time Lords are cast clearly as a force of entropy in *The End of Time:* Rassilon leads them in cheering, "For Gallifrey! For victory! For the end of time itself!"

"Sometimes I think the Time Lord lives too long," the Doctor comments. For Rassilon, revived from the foundation of the Time Lords to lead them to victory, this appears accurate.

> PARTISAN: Perhaps it's time. This is only the furthest edge of the Time War. But at its heart, millions die every second, lost in bloodlust and insanity. With time itself resurrecting them, to find new ways of dying over and over again. A travesty of life. Isn't it better to end it, at last?
> RASSILON: Thank you for your opinion.
> (The Lord President stands and aims his blue metal gauntlet at the Partisan. Energy strikes her, she screams and is atomized.)
> RASSILON: I will not die! Do you hear me? A billion years of Time Lord history riding on our backs. I will not let this perish. I will not! (*The End of Time*)

The Time War

The 2005 revival begins with the revelation that all of the Time Lords have been destroyed in a Time War and only the Doctor remains. Across all of time and space, the Time Lords and Daleks fought, ending in mutual annihilation, all in a time-locked bubble. Russell T Davies introduced the Time War to streamline the Doctor's backstory for new viewers. The Doctor's remorse and isolation afterwards makes him an angrier, more tragic figure than the lighthearted joker of the old series. He is no longer a rebel against authority, but the last survivor of a world he destroyed. "He'd always had a curious relationship with the Time Lords – exile, fugitive, time agent, catspaw and President of the High Council – but Gallifrey was, after all, his home" (Hambly, Kindle Locations 218-219). Now, no longer.

The Doctor is responsible for the war in several ways: the Time Lords send the Fourth Doctor to Skaro to destroy the Daleks just after their creation, but he can't bear to commit genocide (*Genesis of the Daleks*). Also in his fourth incarnation, he is made president of Gallifrey. He constructs the de-mat gun, which had the power to erase its victims from time itself.

Early in the Last Great Time War, Rassilon is resurrected from his tomb in the Dark Tower in the Death Zone (seen in *The Five Doctors*) to lead the Time Lords to battle. He and his followers hatch a scheme to destroy the entire universe and ascend to beings of pure energy outside of creation by using the Ultimate Sanction. This reveals the reason for the Doctor's final strike as they turn nihilistic as the Daleks:

> RASSILON: We will initiate the Final Sanction. The end of time will come at my hand. The rupture will continue until it rips the Time Vortex apart.
> MASTER: That's suicide.
> RASSILON: We will ascend to become creatures of consciousness alone. Free of these bodies, free of time, and cause and effect, while creation itself ceases to be.
> DOCTOR: You see now? That's what they were planning in the final days of the War. I had to stop them. ("The End of Time: Part Two")

They resurrect the Master and implant a signal in him (driving him mad) so they can escape being time-locked. Gallifrey breaks free of the time lock and appears in the skies above Earth, but the Tenth Doctor and the Master stop the plan (*The End of Time*).

As the universe's suffering grows, the Doctor intends to destroy both Time Lords and Daleks by using the Moment, a doomsday weapon that can "sit in judgment" of whoever used it. The Doctor also regenerates into a stronger, more violent man to do what was necessary. This is shown in the 2013 mini-episode "The Night of the Doctor," a prelude to the 50th anniversary special featuring Paul McGann, the Eighth Doctor, as he tries to protect civilians and finally chooses to become the War Doctor. He's aided by the

Sisterhood of Karn who live on another planet of Gallifrey's solar system and protect the Sacred Flame, which produces the Elixir of Life (*The Brain of Morbius*).

The Sontarans tell legends of the Doctor leading Time Lords into battle. Great horrors are created by both sides: The Nightmare Child, the Skaro Degradations, the Army of Meanwhiles and Neverweres led by the Could've Been King, and the Horde of Travesties. The Doctor fires the shot that ends the war – he tells Rose later that all the combatants were "wiped out in one second" ("Dalek"). "He still possesses the Moment, and he'll use it to destroy Daleks and Time Lords alike," a Time Lady notes in "The End of Time: Part Two."

The 50th anniversary special, "The Day of the Doctor" shows fans the last day of the Time War. The War Doctor steals the Moment and takes it to a barn of his childhood near the boarding school he once attended, where it takes on the form of Bad Wolf, a more powerful version of Rose Tyler from the Doctor's near future. The Moment carries the War Doctor to see Ten and Eleven and face who he will become if he destroys Gallifrey. After many adventures battling the Zygons in triplicate, the Tenth and Eleventh meet with the War Doctor, forgiving him and aiding him in his plan. However, with Clara's help, they realize the Moment has brought them together so they can find another course. With the aid of all thirteen incarnations, Gallifrey is saved and hidden in a parallel dimension, while the Daleks destroy themselves in the crossfire. In "The Time of the Doctor," the Gallifreyans send him another set of regenerations and he resolves to go looking for them.

Doctors, Companions, and their Personalities

First Doctor (William Hartnell)

The First Doctor has said in the show that he is the "original" incarnation of the character (*The Five Doctors*). While arrogant and short-tempered, he is also fatherly and compassionate, if a trifle condescending. He is the one to discover the Daleks, and of course, interest viewers in *Doctor Who* in his tenure from 1963 through 1966.

He begins his story by fleeing from Gallifrey to earth in a stolen and malfunctioning TARDIS, from where he and his companions embark on many adventures. He dresses in an Edwardian black frock coat with long white hair. "Hartnell's frock coat and Dickensian attitude make him seem a refugee from the world of Conan Doyle, gaslight, hansom cabs, imperial adventure and Jack the Ripper" (Newman 16). He is also fond of a blue crystal signet ring. He is heard to say, "I am a citizen of the universe, and a gentleman to boot!" Frail and steadily growing weaker through his battle with Cybermen in Antarctica (*The Tenth Planet*), the Doctor announces he's "growing thin," lies down, and regenerates.

Companions

The Doctor's granddaughter Susan Foreman (Carole Ann Ford) is living with him on earth and attending school when the first episode begins. In the original pilot, Susan was a traveler from the forty-ninth century in futuristic clothes unrelated to the Doctor – the final script writer, Anthony Coburn, suggested Susan be the Doctor's granddaughter for children to have an easier time relating to the relationship (Haining 19-21). As her parents are never seen or clearly mentioned (only that the Doctor has had children before), it's possible Susan calls him that only as a term of endearment. Susan says she's "in [her] sixteenth year," though this may be a lie as well (*The Roof of the World*).

Carole Ann Ford, her actress, says, "Susan was originally going to be quite a tough little girl – a bit like the *Avengers* lady, using judo and karate – but having telepathic communication with the Doctor. Then they decided they wanted me to be a normal teenage girl so that other teenage girls could easily identify with me" (Tulloch and Alvarado 210). Her role thus became far more conventional. She adds that "I think they chose me because they wanted a good screamer. I did an awful lot of that" (Haining 81). She is the first companion to leave – she falls in love with a human and the Doctor locks her out of the TARDIS, forcing her to choose love over him.

SUSAN: Grandfather!
DOCTOR [OC]: Listen, Susan, please. I've double-locked the doors. You can't get in. Now move back, child, where I can see you.
DOCTOR: During all the years, I've been taking care of you, you in return have been taking care of me.
SUSAN [on scanner]: Oh, Grandfather, I belong with you!
DOCTOR: Not any longer, Susan. You're still my grandchild and always will be, but now, you're a woman too.
[Riverside]
DOCTOR [OC]: I want you to belong somewhere, to have roots of your own. With David, you'll be able to find those roots and live normally like any woman should do.
[TARDIS]
DOCTOR: Believe me, my dear, your future lies with David, and not with a silly old buffer like me. One day, I shall come back. Yes, I shall come back. Until then, there must be no regrets, no tears, no anxieties. Just go forward in all your beliefs, and prove to me that I am not mistaken in mine. Goodbye, Susan, goodbye, my dear.

[Riverside]
(The TARDIS dematerializes). (*The Dalek Invasion of Earth*)

Later, the Doctor describes himself as "the last of the Time Lords," suggesting Susan has died. If he ever returns for her, this scene has not been recorded.

Barbara and Ian, Susan's two teachers, follow her home one day, trying to puzzle out the girl who knows advanced science but has no idea about British coinage. They stumble into the TARDIS in a junkyard, and it sweeps them off on adventures with the Doctor and Susan.

Barbara Wright (played by Jacqueline Hill), is a history teacher to aid the historical program Doctor Who was meant to be. She argues constantly with the Doctor, unlike many wimpier companions that follow, saying, "You treat everybody and everything as something less important than yourself." (*An Unearthly Child*). Mostly, she demands they interfere and change history.

> FIRST DOCTOR: No, Barbara! Ian agrees with me. He's got to escort the victim to the altar... they've made him a warrior, and he's promised me not to interfere with the sacrifice. Barbara: Well, they've made me a goddess. And I forbid it!... There'll be no sacrifice this afternoon. The reincarnation of Yetaxa will prove to the people that you don't need to sacrifice a human being in order to make it rain!
> ...You can't rewrite history. Not one line!...Barbara, one last appeal. What you are trying to do is utterly impossible! I know. Believe me, I know!
> BARBARA: Not "Barbara." Yetaxa. (*The Aztecs*)

In her mid-thirties, Barbara is the oldest female companion until Sarah Jane's return. Hill adds, "The good thing about Barbara was that because she was older than most of the girls since, the writers were more hesitant about making her look silly, or scream too much. That side of things was largely left to Carole Ann Ford, which is why she left earlier than Bill Russell and myself" (*Doctor Who Interviews*).

Ian Chesterton is the story's young action hero. He's impetuous and brave, the one called on to fight when such things are necessary. Unable to return home, Ian and Barbara risk travel in a Dalek time ship and successfully reach 1960s London, two years after their departure (*The Chase*). While the pair aren't strictly romantic on the show, they get married after they leave the Doctor. Sarah Jane mentions on her own show that Barbara and Ian became professors at Cambridge but had not aged since the 1960s (*Death of the Doctor*). Later, Ian becomes the Chairman of the Governors for the school where he once taught, Coal Hill Secondary School. By this time, Clara Oswald, teaches here as well (*The Day of the Doctor*).

Vicki, Katarina, and Dodo follow Susan as the replacement "young woman," or perhaps, "young screamer." One critic lumps together "Jo, Dodo, and Susan, whiners, shriekers, and mini-skirted little girls with no apparent individual willpower, no recognizable backbone, and no Valkyrie Reflex" (Burke 176).

Vicki is the first companion the Doctor asks to travel with him on the show. About sixteen, she's a genius on a futuristic planet – By the age of 10 she had obtained certificates in medicine, physics, computers, chemistry, and other sciences. Barbara kills Vicki's pet sand beast, thinking it a monster, but the two soon reconcile. However, Maureen O'Brian (Vicki) notes: "I found the role limiting to say the least...to look frightened and scream a lot is not very demanding to an actor" (Tulloch and Alvarado 210).

Steven Taylor (Peter Purves), a pilot on Flight Red Fiftyfar in the future, crashes on the planet Mechanus. Stranded there for some time, he has only a toy panda named HiFi for company. He stows away on the TARDIS when it visits (*The Chase*). Steven and Vikki enjoy adventures on the TARDIS, as young adventurers from the future (in contrast with homesick Barbara and Ian). Steven stays on through the loss of several female companions, though he begins to question the Doctor on the pointlessness of their deaths.

Eventually, he leaves to help rebuild a civilization, though on a world far from his own (*The Savages*).

In *The Myth Makers*, Vicki falls in love with Troilus at Troy, and stays with him as his Cressida. She tells Troilus: "The main thing is I belong here now with you. If you'll have me....There's only us now" (*The Myth Makers*). The Doctor replaces her with the Trojan priestess Katarina (Adrienne Hill), but Katrina is too primitive, understanding little of science or technology. "She was really a very simple girl, lost once she was taken out of her ancient world into the high technology of the TARDIS," actress Adrienne Hill reports (Haining 85). On her first episode as companion, a man tries to take her hostage. Screaming incessantly, she hits the outer door controls and becomes the first companion ever to die.

> STEVEN: She pressed the wrong button, Doctor.
> DOCTOR: She may have wanted to, dear boy. She wanted to save our lives.
> BRET: It must have been quick.
> DOCTOR: I hope she's reached her Place of Perfection.
> STEVEN: Yes, but not that way.
> DOCTOR: She didn't understand. She couldn't understand. She wanted to save our lives and perhaps the lives of all the other beings of the Solar System. I hope she's found her Perfection. Oh, how I shall always remember her as one of the Daughters of the Gods. Yes, as one of the Daughters of the Gods. (*The Daleks' Master Plan*)

Sara Kingdom (Jean Marsh) is generally given the status of companion. She is the first of a new type, appearing in a black catsuit and described as "Ruthless, hard, efficient" (*The Daleks' Master Plan*). As a Space Security Service (SSS) agent, she's armed and dangerous...and determined to defeat the Doctor. In fact, she was created for a possible spinoff, but this didn't come to pass. "She plays a different kind of companion, one more outwardly aggressive and cool than many of the others seen thus far...however, as the 'bad girl' she could not be allowed to live" (Muir 120). She's caught in the field of the Time Destructor and hyper-aged to the point of death.

Dodo Chaplet (Jackie Lane) runs into a police box and gets carried off (a humorous introduction that befalls several companions). She resembles and imitates Susan, whose part she once auditioned for. "Dodo was to be a close replacement of Susan, a surrogate granddaughter for the Doctor" (Tulloch and Alvarado 210). She's so naïve that on her first adventure, she doesn't even realize she's on an alien planet:

> STEVEN: Just where do you think you're going?
> DODO: Out.
> STEVEN: Out?
> DODO: Yes, I thought I'd get some fresh air. Somebody opened the door and...
> STEVEN: But nobody said you could go out.
> DODO: Do they have to then?
> STEVEN: Well, of course they do. Look, Dodo, you don't know what you might have found out here. No gravity, poisoned atmosphere, all sorts of things. Look, stop prancing around over there. What happens if you get lost?
> DODO: I catch a bus back. (*The Ark*)

She parts from the Doctor off-screen as her new friend Polly explains, "She says she's feeling much better and she'd like to stay here in London, and she sends you her love." The Doctor dismisses her with an annoyed, "Her love? Oh, there's gratitude for you. Take her all the way around the world, through space and time, and then..." (*The War Machines*). He flies off with Polly and her friend Ben in tow in Dodo's place.

Polly Wright (Anneke Wills) is a 1960's rockabilly companion, who picks up the manly sailor Ben Jackson (Michael Craze) in a bar. Ben calls her "our little dolly-rocker Duchess" ("*The Smugglers*"). Her actress says, "I thought it would be a very good idea to play a total coward. Television was full of brave ladies in those days. I wanted to play a sort of feminine anti-hero, a weedy, frightened lady who screamed and kicked and shouted 'Doctor' at the least sign of danger" (Haining 87-88).

Polly and Ben also preside over the First Doctor's regeneration. When they reach Polly and Ben's time, they depart (as many companions of the time are accidental or searching for home in an unreliable TARDIS). The Doctor dismisses them with, "Off you go. Now go on, Ben can catch his ship and become an Admiral, and you Polly, you can look after Ben" (*The Faceless Ones*). In 2010, Sarah Jane Smith says Ben and Polly are running an orphanage together in India (*Death of the Doctor*).

Second Doctor (Patrick Troughton)

Playing a recorder and bumbling about in an over-large frock coat and bowtie (to say nothing of a giant fur on occasion), the Second Doctor was considered quite clownish and irreverent. Many saw him as the impish uncle or an escaped Marx Brother or Stooge rather than the stern but whimsical grandfather. He was reckless but also ruthless: to defeat the Cybermen, he wired a set of tomb doors to fatally electrocute anyone who opened them (*The Tomb of the Cybermen*). He was lighthearted and popular, a happy teammate for his companions.

Companions

Jamie upon seeing an airplane at Gatwick Airport cries, "Ooh, it's a flyin' beastie!" (*The Faceless Ones*). Jamie McCrimmon (played by Fraser Hines from 1966 – 1969) is recruited from the Jacobite Rebellion at Culloden Moor, Scotland, in 1746. While Katrina is hopelessly lost on the TARDIS, Jaime, age 22, proves quite clever and adaptable. He often sticks with his red kilt and sporran, though he occasionally wears more modern clothes. Brave in dangerous situations and loving towards several female companions, he is the Second Doctor's longest companion, and one of the most popular of all time. Jaime, Two, and Six also work together in the special *The Two Doctors*.

Victoria Waterfield (Deborah Watling) returns to the young, childlike, screamers. Upon seeing a painting of her, Jaime sets out on a desperate rescue mission to save the sweet Victorian girl from the Daleks. Watling notes: "I was first seen in *Doctor Who* screaming at the Daleks, and I think I continued screaming for the next year. I screamed myself hoarse at every monster that came in sight" (Haining 90). Worn from her terrifying adventures, she leaves in *Fury from the Deep*.

> SECOND DOCTOR: You look very nice in that dress, Victoria.
> VICTORIA: Thank you. Don't you think it's a bit...
> SECOND DOCTOR: A bit short? Oh, I shouldn't worry about that. Look at Jamie's. (*Tomb of the Cybermen*)

The next companion, Zoe Heriot (Wendy Padbury) stands out far more. "A genius astrophysicist in a silver catsuit from a 21st century space-station, Zoe has class and sass combined, Dr. Who's closest equivalent to the *Avengers'* Emma Peel" (Martin). She's also as scientifically gifted and intuitive as the Doctor himself:

> DOCTOR: I'm going to take the test. I can't let you go in there alone! What do I do?
> ZOE: Oh, sit down. And put this headset on. And press the button. Press the button!
> DOCTOR: All right, there's no need to shout! Now go away and don't fuss me. No, come back. What's this? It's all right, I know. Right, fire away. I'm ready.
> (Zoe gestures at him to press the button. The circling symbols come up but he doesn't manage to get them into coherent equations.)
> ZOE: Oh. Doctor, you've got it all wrong.
> DOCTOR: Oh dear, I've been working in square roots. Can I have that again, please?
> ZOE: Well they don't give you a second shots. Well, press the button again.
> SELRIS: This is the most advanced machine. Perhaps he can't answer the questions.

ZOE: Of course he can. The Doctor's almost as clever as I am. (*The Krotons*)

The trio made a wonderful and popular team. While working for BBC, John Nathan-Turner (future *Doctor Who* producer) noted: "There was a tremendous atmosphere of naughty schoolboys, almost, with the last Pat Troughton and Frazer Hines and Wendy Padbury all goofing around" (*Doctor Who Interviews*).

The Second Doctor's ending is ignominious and heart-rending. The Time Lords arrest him for interfering with other cultures and forcibly regenerate him. They also banish him to earth, disabling his TARDIS. Zoe and Jaime are mindwiped and returned to their times, with no memory of the Doctor's adventures (*The War Games*). He returns in *The Three Doctors*, *The Five Doctors*, and *The Two Doctors* (with Six).

Third Doctor (Jon Pertwee)

In the seventh season, it was decided to shoot in color, and to save on money and shake up the premise, the creators decided to strand the Doctor on Earth. Thus he would work for UNIT, with more characters to take some of the action, in the fan-familiar world of 1970s Britain.

This Doctor was flamboyant in dress, with an Inverness cape, frilled shirts, velvet smoking jackets, and bright cravats. These were in fashion at the time but also a statement of his boldness and adventuring nature. He defended himself, rather than needing a male companion to always do the stunts. He also drove a beloved Edwardian roadster named Bessie when the TARDIS was unavailable. He had many more gadgets, and modified the sonic screwdriver to have many additional uses.

The Third Doctor stood out in the flamboyant and overly-colorful seventies by dressing even more outrageously – he was known for velvet smoking jackets, ruffled poet shirts, a black silk cravat, and even a sweeping cape, like a mediaeval troubadour racing through England in his bright yellow car, Bessie. His old fashioned dress offered an aristocratic look and also linked him to John Steed of the terribly popular *The Avengers,* famous for the then-out-of-date bowler hat. (Frankel, *What, Where, & How* 66-67)

THIRD DOCTOR: My goodness, no. Don't you realise that when I was stranded on this little planet of yours, I had nothing but these clothes that I Oh, my goodness!
LIZ: What is it, Doctor?
THIRD DOCTOR: Well, I've just realised. I don't even own these. I borrowed them from the hospital. And there's that car, too. Yes, you know, I took to that car. It had character.
BRIGADIER: No, Doctor. That car must be returned to its owner.
THIRD DOCTOR: Must it? Yes, yes, I suppose it must. Still, there's no reason why you couldn't find me something similar, is there? I mean, it could persuade me to stay, you know.
BRIGADIER: Oh, very well.
THIRD DOCTOR: Good. When can we go and choose it?
BRIGADIER: Not yet. I must arrange for a full set of papers first. By the way, I've just realised. I don't even know your name.
THIRD DOCTOR: Smith. Doctor *John* Smith. (*Spearhead from Space*)

A James-Bond-style agent and something of a rebellious maverick for UNIT, he is forced into conflict with his arch-nemesis, the Master, over and over. He also goes on occasional missions for the Time Lords.

Finally, the villainous Omega from a universe of anti-matter attacks. The Doctor joins previous incarnations of himself to defeat him, and as a reward, the Doctor's exile is lifted (*The Three Doctors*). After this, he and Jo, then Sarah Jane, adventure in time and space once more.

The Doctor and UNIT investigate a retreat run by Tibetan monks and discover a colony of monstrous spiders linked to the blue planet Metebelis III. To save his companions, his old mentor, K'anpo Rimpoche, and the whole cosmos from the spiders, the Third Doctor absorbs lethal levels of radiation to destroy the spiders' web and sacrifices his life (*Planet of the Spiders*). As he dies dramatically before Sarah Jane and Lethbridge-Stewart, K'anpo Rimpoche's psychic projection appears and promises the Time Lord will return, giving him "a little push" to begin regeneration.

Companions

Brigadier Sir Alistair Gordon Lethbridge-Stewart is a founder of UNIT and one of the closest friends of the Doctor. Nonetheless, he represents the military head of UNIT, and he and the Doctor often disagree. As the Third Doctor says of him, "He's hidebound, you see. He always does everything by the rules. I keep telling him. I said, there are times, you know, when you've simply got to cut right through the red tape" (*Frontier in Space*). Defending earth from the Great Intelligence, the Brigadier meets the Second Doctor in *The Web of Fear*. After the next regeneration, the Brigadier appoints the Doctor UNIT's full-time scientific advisor.

Stuck at UNIT on earth, the Third and Fourth Doctors work for the Brigadier to keep earth safe. In fact, thanks to *The Five Doctors* and *Adventures in Time*, the Brigadier works with all the original Doctors, returning for the Seventh Doctor in *Battlefield*. He also appears on *The Sarah Jane Adventures*, and Eleven tries to contact him in "Closing Time." His daughter appears (and references him) in New Who's "The Power of Three," "The Day of the Doctor" and "Death in Heaven." In fact, the reimagined Brigadier returns in the last of these. As such, he somehow appears with every Doctor except Eight through Ten.

The Brigadier is courageous and controlled, even in the most outlandish situations. In *The Daemons*, confronted by a living gargoyle animated with demonic power, he says simply, "Chap with the wings there. Five rounds rapid." The second sentence was also the name of the actor's autobiography.

The Third Doctor's other new companion is a cool-minded scientist and a professor at Cambridge, Liz Shaw

(Caroline John). The Brigadier describes her as "An expert in meteorites, degrees in medicine, physics and a dozen other subjects" (*Spearhead from Space*). While she's a scientist, she's also something of a secretary, sounding board, and babysitter for the Doctor as she promises to look after him as well as liaising with UNIT. Her actress notes, "They would insist on dressing me in mini-skirts and not a lot else. I used to point out that these sorts of clothes would hardly have been Liz Shaw, Cambridge scientist's kind of wardrobe, but I think they were a bit too scared there would be trouble if the traditional 'Doctor Who' glamour girl was dispensed with" (*Doctor Who Interviews*).

She tries to balance capability and arrogance but doesn't always succeed:

> BRIGADIER: May I remind you, Miss Shaw, that you're still a serving member of UNIT? I don't entirely care for your tone.
> LIZ: I don't much care for yours either. No wonder the Doctor cleared off. (*Inferno*)

She came across too cold and too knowledgeable to be dependent on the Doctor. "Unfortunately, the writers seemingly did not know how to develop a believable relationship between the Doctor and a female companion who did not require rescue" Muir adds (177). In fact, Liz's character complains that all the Doctor needs was "someone to pass him his test tubes and tell him how brilliant he was" (*Terror of the Autons*). Thus, Liz vanishes after just four episodes.

Her replacement, Jo Grant (Katy Manning) is far different. Her character is clumsy and incompetent though somewhat endearing: In her first appearance, she sprays the Doctor's project with a fire extinguisher and costs him three months' work. He calls her a "ham-fisted bungler" and greets her announcement that she's his new assistant with a plaintive, "Oh no!" With her mid-length blonde hair, fluffy pastel sweaters, and belief in astrology, she's a product of her decade. Still, she has some talents, especially escaping with her special skeleton key. She knows karate and can pilot a helicopter. Critics are divided on her effectiveness.

> Jo's role throughout this series can look oddly uneven from both perspectives. In *Day of the Daleks,* she fetches and carries for the Doctor and for UNIT, is fearful of ghosts and seems naively trusting when the twenty-second century Controller tells her how wonderful life is. She arrives on Peladon in a posh frock and hairdo, ready for her date with Mike Yates. She spends a great deal of time in *The Mutants* being captured, rescued, captured again, swept up in the arms of a good-looking hero. In *The Time Monster,* she mostly tags along after the Doctor, to Cambridge and to Atlantis, where she's promptly sent off for another groovy frock and glam hairdo. It's so in keeping with 1972's expectations, and so alien to a modern viewer. (Lotz, Kindle Locations 1891-1896).

In the environmentally-minded *The Green Death*, she falls for Professor Clifford Jones, an activist and substitute Doctor.

> JONES: My dear good child, I've got work to do.
> JO: You're being patronizing.
> JONES: Aye, so I am. But I've still got work to do.

She leaves UNIT and the Doctor to marry and live happily ever after. Her character returns for the Doctor's funeral in *The Sarah Jane Adventures,* and she describes a wonderful life of children and wild adventure on earth.

Mike Yates, a young UNIT officer, also joins the Doctor on adventures. He is friendly with Liz Shaw and appears attracted to Jo Grant. In *The Green Death*, he's hypnotized and forced to shoot the Doctor. The Doctor saves him, but the devastated Yates chooses to retire.

The Third Doctor's last companion, who transitions to the next Doctor, is the beloved Sarah Jane Smith (Elisabeth Sladen). Introduced as a journalist, she challenges the Doctor and demands he answer her questions properly:

SARAH: What's that?
DOCTOR: That's my alarm clock.
SARAH: Oh Doctor, kindly don't be so patronising. Now what is it really?
DOCTOR: It's a rhondium sensor. It detects delta particles. At a preset spectrum density of fifteen ams, it oscillates this little cylinder there, which promotes a vacuum in there which wakes me up. Clear?
SARAH: Well, why do you want to be woken up when it detects delta particles?
DOCTOR: Because I'm very fond of delta particles. Why do you ask so many questions?
SARAH: Because I'm a journalist. (*The Time Warrior*)

Sarah Jane begins the show by rescuing the Doctor. She's unexpectedly yanked back to the past on her first adventure, but finds herself giving orders to medieval men and aliens alike. "If I had an army of girls such as you, I might hold this castle forever," on medieval inhabitant notes (*The Time Warrior*). She's a women's lib companion with her speeches, but one far more colorful than Liz Shaw:

SARAH: I'm not afraid of men. They don't own the world. Why should women always have to cook and carry for them?
MEG: What else should we do?
SARAH: Stand up for ourselves. Tell the men you're tired of working for them like slaves.
MEG: We are slaves.
SARAH: Then you should set yourselves free…You're still living in the Middle Ages. (*The Time Warrior*)

"It was important that my character had a life – and subplots – of her own and wasn't just arm candy. It was imperative not to agree with the male characters out of habit. Decisions had to be questioned – even the Doctor's" her actress explains (Sladen 165). In fact, given dull screaming parts, Sladen began to rework them. "I began to alter the odd word, then sentences, then whole exchanges. I'd never ask, I'd just do it" (110).

Fourth Doctor (Tom Baker)

The Fourth Doctor (Tom Baker) lasted for a decade and was many fans' favorite Doctor and gateway to the series. Under his reign, the show reached 100 million viewers around the world in 37 countries (Kistler 138). The actor would walk about in character, insisting that he was undercover, in order to maintain his fans' sense of wonder.

Meanwhile his character is crowned President of Gallifrey, and partnered with one of the most popular all-time companions, Sarah Jane Smith, as well as the only Time Lady companion, Romana. Many of his episodes are adaptations of Gothic classics, from *Frankenstein* to *The Mummy*. He is best known for his incredibly long colorful scarf, though he also has a brown coat, fedora, and occasional costumes. "His coat would subtly change color depending on the genre of the particular serial – yellow-brown for adventure, red for action, and grey for horror or mystery" (Frankel, *What, Where, & How* 66). He uses the scarf in many ways, from traps to combat, though essentially a nonviolent person. He is goofier than many other Doctors, saying, "Well, of course I'm being childish! There's no point being grown-up if you can't be childish sometimes" (*Robots*) and constantly offering jelly babies about. He pulls occasional pranks as well. He is also quite intolerant of authority figures as the Time Lords continued to run his life.

On Logopolis, saving the universe, he falls from the Pharos Project telescope and joins hands with a vision of himself in order to regenerate. The scarf is unraveled by the Fifth Doctor in the beginning of his regeneration.

In 1983, Baker declined to appear in *The Five Doctors*, feeling it was too soon, and his punting scenes from the lost episode *Shada* were added in his place. He appeared in the thirtieth anniversary and twenty-eight years after leaving the show, began recording new audio adventures with Big Finish.

Companions

Sarah and the Doctor achieve the status of best friends, not grandparent and grandchild or master and pupil. As the Doctor grows comfortable in their dynamic, he learns to exploit it and push Sarah's buttons: In *The Ark in Space*, Sarah is trapped, and the Doctor begins castigating her:

> SARAH: I'm jammed. I can't move forward or back.
> DOCTOR [OC]: Oh, stop whining, girl. You're useless.
> SARAH: Oh, Doctor.
> DOCTOR: Oh, Doctor. Is that all you can say for yourself?
> Stupid, foolish girl. We should never have relied on you. I knew
> you'd let us down. That's the trouble with girls like you. You
> think you're tough, but when you're really up against it, you've
> no guts at all.
> (Sarah manages to pull herself forward again.)

When Sarah succeeds through his reverse psychology, the Doctor confesses he was only "encouraging" her and adds, "You've done marvelously, Sarah. I'm very proud of you. I really am very proud of you." Her occasional partner, Royal Navy surgeon Harry Sullivan, is by contrast far more inept.

> LESTER: Harry, don't touch it. Open that buckle and you'll
> be blown to kingdom come.
> HARRY: You mean it's booby trapped?
> LESTER: These buckles can't be opened until the
> Cybermen beam the release signal.
> DOCTOR: Harry, were you trying to undo this?
> HARRY: Well, naturally.
> DOCTOR: Did you make the rocks fall, Harry?
> HARRY: Er, well, I suppose I must have done, yes.
> (The Doctor laughs.)
> DOCTOR: Harry Sullivan is an imbecile!
> (And he passes out again.) (*Revenge of the Cybermen*)

After Harry moves on, Sarah begins the buddy pairing of one Doctor and one female companion, rather than a larger group. The Fourth Doctor in turn travels singly with Leela and Romana afterward, and the 2005 reboot is based on the Doctor-single companion partnership.

After Sarah Jane Smith, Leela the warrior-savage (Louise Jameson) arrives. She is a primitive, superstitious cave girl, a strong woman, but one in a scanty outfit with plenty of cleavage. The Doctor meets her on a planet colonized by the Mordee centuries before, where he is worshipped as a god (*The Face of Evil*). She displays a single-minded ignorance when speaking with the Doctor:

> DOCTOR: You'll upset the dog. Listen, Leela, you simply must stop attacking people.
> LEELA: Why?
> DOCTOR: Because you'll get us into trouble.
> LEELA: Do not worry, Doctor. I shall protect you. (*Image of the Fendahl*)

> Throughout the season, the Doctor's relationship with Leela is broadly based on a professor and pupil footing, with the Doctor seeking to "tame her savage heart" (in the opening episode of The Invisible Enemy, she is pictured carefully writing her name on the blackboard). This paternalistic aspect is made slightly more palatable by the fact that Leela is aware of the Doctor's attempts at "civilizing" her, and uses or loses what she deems valuable - she acknowledges the benefits of science, but balances this with her instinct. That said, there's a tetchiness to their relationship, replete with wince-inducing moments when he ridicules her for being "primitive," "savage" or just plain stupid. (Lotz, Kindle Locations 1130-1136)

The Doctor visits the Bi-Al Foundation medical center in the year 5000, where he saves the locals from a Swarm. Professor Marius gives his mechanical dog, K9, to the Doctor in this episode (*The Invisible Enemy*). K9, one of the most beloved companions, was difficult to control and film but a favorite with children and adults.

In *The Invasion of Time*, Leela decides to stay on Gallifrey for a conventional marriage. K9 stays as well (while K9 reappears as K9 Mark II, Leela's final fate in the Time War is unknown).

> ROMANA: My name is Romanadvoratnelundar.

45

DOCTOR: I'm so sorry about that. Is there anything we can do? (*The Ribos Operation*)

On his next mission, to find the six-part "Key to Time" in a full season arc, the Doctor is given the Time Lady Romana (Mary Tamm) as an "assistant." As he protests, "In my experience, assistants mean trouble. I have to protect them and show them and teach them and couldn't I just, couldn't I just manage with K9?" (*The Ribos Operation*). She's an "ice queen" and scientist, tall and lovely in a long white gown, fur coat, and sparkling tiara. "Cool (naturally for an Ice Queen) intellectual, and ironic, Romana I became almost a female Doctor, lacking only the Doctor's vast experience and considerable skills of situational improvisation" (Layton 106). She's younger than the Doctor ("nearly 140" to the Doctor's 700-plus) and did better on her tests but lacks real-world experience. Nonetheless, she flies the TARDIS "by the book" and does everything possible to aggravate the Doctor. "Unfortunately, many Doctor Who viewers found Mary Tamm too aggressive as Romana. They were not yet ready for a companion of her stature" (Muir 270).

DOCTOR: Now, listen. It's no good, this isn't going to work.
ROMANA: Doctor, you're not giving me a chance. It's funny, you know, but before I met you, I was even willing to be impressed.
DOCTOR: Indeed.
ROMANA: Oh yes. Of course, now I realise that your behaviour simply derives from a subtransitory experiential hypertoid induced condition, aggravated, I expect, by multi-encephalogical tensions.
DOCTOR: What's that supposed to mean?
ROMANA: Well, to put it very simply, Doctor, you're suffering from a massive compensation syndrome.
DOCTOR: Is that the sort of rubbish they're pouring into your head at the Academy?
ROMANA: Do you know, I might even use your case in my thesis when I'm back on Gallifrey. (*The Ribos Operation*)

Romana soon regenerates with a new actress and new personality. In fact, she cycles through several faces then chooses Princess Astra whom they met in the previous episode. Fans are divided on whether she's more skilled at regenerating than the Doctor, or whether she uses technology (or holographic projections) to make this possible. The new Romana is sweeter, and she and the Doctor share some sparks. "A small, laughing, effervescent figure," Romana II is more of a traditional companion than her previous incarnation (Haining 102). The actress, Lalla Ward, explains, "My Romana was a contrast to the first one because it was felt the Doctor got on better with someone who didn't seem stuck up" (Haining 102).

On Alzarius, a planet with Gallifrey's coordinates in the strange universe of E-Space, the Doctor meets a precocious, orphaned boy named Adric (Matthew Waterhouse) who stows away (*Full Circle*). Meanwhile, Romana and K9 stay in E-Space to help the oppressed Tharils (*Warrior's Gate*). In the audio adventures, Romana becomes president of Gallifrey and teams up with Leela, each guarded by their own K9.

> DOCTOR: There's bound to be an awful lot of fuss about Romana. Why she stayed in E-space, official investigations, that sort of thing.
> ADRIC: The Time Lords won't approve?
> DOCTOR: What? She has broken the cardinal rule of Gallifrey. She has become involved, and in a pretty permanent sort of way. I think that you and I should let a few oceans flow under a few bridges before we head back home.
> ADRIC: So we don't get to go to Gallifrey.
> DOCTOR: Yes. Let me put another question to you. I have a place in mind that's on the way, well, more or less, give or take a parsec or two. It's my home from home. It's called Earth. (*Logopolis*)

Eighteen-year-old Matthew Waterhouse was a big fan with no formal acting training, who gushed, "Less than a year ago, I was sitting three A-levels at school and taking time off from revision to watch *Doctor Who*. Now I'm rehearsing with Tom Baker, Lalla Ward and K9 and joining the series" (Haining 196). K9 finally left the show in 1980, as the producers said he was too clever and always had all the answers. A nation of fans went into mourning with massive campaigns and protests. Nonetheless the dog was cut.

Back in N-space, the normal universe, the Doctor visits the Traken Union. He meets the gentle Nyssa of Traken (Sarah Sutton) and her father Tremas, the Keeper. It's soon discovered that the Master is trying to steal lifeforce to get a new body. The Doctor attempts to kill the Master, but the Master escapes in Tremas's body (*The Keeper of Traken*). On visiting Logopolis, the Doctor finds that the modern-day human Tegan Jovanka (Janet Fielding) has accidently boarded, seeking an actual police box. He meets Nyssa once more and discovers a mysterious Watcher, actually his future self. The Master attempts to destroy the universe, but the Doctor saves it at the cost of his life – the Watcher's presence has alerted him that death was near (*Logopolis*).

Fifth Doctor (Peter Davison)

The Fifth Doctor is gentler, more hesitant, and younger than the others. His actor, Peter Davison said, "I would like to be more down-to-earth. We thought we needed something English and more youthful. I'm going to be a more heroic Doctor Who!" (Haining 204). The character is fascinated by Victorian and Edwardian England, down to his constant cricket uniform, which remains in place for most episodes:

> The first four Doctors have a style but not a specific costume: when in Tibet, Troughton wore a shaggy fur coat, for instance; and even Pertwee has a wardrobe of different frilly shirts, velvet jackets, and caped ulsters. From the middle of Tom Baker's tenure, each Doctor unvaryingly sports their own distinctive, question-mark-pocked uniform as if dressing up as themselves. It's a comic-book convention, unsustainable in live-action where audiences wonder if the hero is indeed wearing the same never-

cleaned, never-worn-out clothes for years on end.
(Newman 97)

The producers proposed this, in order to make it easy for fans to buy licensed costume pieces. Only by the time of the reboot did the Doctors begin dressing in a variety of outfits once more.

Five also is known for the sprig of celery in his lapel, which he eats to save himself from poisoned gas in his final story, *The Caves of Androzani*. (Later on, the Eleventh Doctor asks for celery after being tortured by a Silurian in "Cold Blood"). Davison stayed for three years or 74 episodes, the shortest-lived Doctor at the time.

Much later, the Fifth Doctor appeared in the short film "Time Crash" with the Tenth.

> In the minisode "Time Crash" the Fifth Doctor is annoyed, believing his counterpart to be a fan who has broken into the TARDIS, and complains about the fan groups popping up everywhere. In turn, the Tenth Doctor gushes like a fan (which he actually is) at seeing the Fifth. He notes, "You were *my* Doctor," something often heard from the mobs at conventions. As viewers watch, they're not sure if David Tennant is gushing over Peter Davison or the Tenth Doctor is gushing over the Fifth, or both at once. (Frankel, *What Where & How* 59)

Peter Davison is actually David Tennant's father-in-law. Tennant's wife appears as "the Doctor's Daughter" in the episode of that name.

Companions

In *Castrovalva*, Four's regeneration grows problematic, and the new Doctor must fight to heal while also rescuing Adric from the Master with Tegan and Nyssa's help. They become a traveling foursome: Aggressive Tegan who is miserable at the Doctor's failure to take her home, the sweet and quiet Nyssa, and the often-arrogant whiz kid Adric.

> FIFTH DOCTOR: Well, there's a probability of anything. Statistically speaking, if you gave typewriters to a treeful of monkeys, they'd eventually produce the works of William Shakespeare.
> NYSSA: [trying to draw the Doctor's attention away from his conversation with Tegan to the approaching craft on the viewscreen] Doctor...
> FIFTH DOCTOR: Of course, you and I both know that at the end of a millennium they'd still be tapping out gibberish.
> TEGAN: And you'd be tapping it out right alongside them. I only asked you a simple question. (*Mawdryn Undead*)

Nyssa, while literally a teenager in a tiara, is also a scientist and intellectual. Sarah Sutton (Nyssa) says: "Nyssa is very technical and she's very bright and she's adventurous..." She's also a telepathic alien, sensitive and in tune with the universe" (Tulloch and Alvarado 222). By contrast, "Tegan the independent 1981 'cosmopolitan' professional lady" is more straightforward, a tough, seasoned Australian and typical woman of contemporary earth" (Tulloch and Alvarado 211). She's also reminiscent of Sarah Jane "like her an aggressive, impulsive 'professional'" (Tulloch and Alvarado 218).

> VANESSA: Oh, please, dear, do let's get a man from the garage.
> TEGAN: No way. The stories I've heard about the way they exploit helpless women. You want the job done well, you do it yourself, that's what Dad used to say.
> VANESSA: Perhaps some knight errant will stop for us.
> TEGAN: You have to learn to fend for yourself in the outback, you know.
> VANESSA: Your father's farm is hardly the outback, my dear, and neither is this. You know, I can see a garage not even a quarter of a mile away.
> TEGAN: Industry and application, Aunt Vanessa. Air stewardesses are supposed to be resourceful. (*Logopolis*)

Her actress adds, "Tegan is young, bright, brash and assertive and she's not at all afraid of putting the Doctor in his place. She tends to charge in without thinking at times, but deep down she's a very caring person" (Haining 202).

Adric is almost the only companion to die (Katrina and Sara Kingdom were only companions for a multipart episode each). His death shocks fans across the world as he sacrifices himself to save his friends in *Earthshock*.

Mark Strickson plays Turlough, the companion who is also a traitor. On one of the Doctor's adventures, he helps resolve a time paradox and befriends Tegan and Nyssa, finally invited to join the Doctor in his travels (*Mawdryn Undead*). Working for the Black Guardian, he actually tries to kill the Doctor. He later reforms, accepting his role as a protector of others and spending the rest of his life helping the population of Sarn (*Planet of Fire*). Turlough, despite his status as a Trion political prisoner, brings the survivors of an attack by the Master to his home planet, as he's finally allowed back.

Tegan leaves quite abruptly in *Resurrection of the Daleks*. It's not integrated well into the plot – she "simply has a temper tantrum and says she has seen too much violence" (Muir 339).

> TEGAN: No. It's just I don't think I can go on.
> FIFTH DOCTOR: You want to stay on Earth?
> TEGAN: My aunt Vanessa said, when I became an air stewardess, if you stop enjoying it, give it up.
> FIFTH DOCTOR: Tegan...
> TEGAN: It's stopped being fun, Doctor. Goodbye. *[Shakes the Doctor's hand]* Turlough. *[Shakes Turlough's hand]*
> TURLOUGH: Goodbye.
> TEGAN: I'll miss you both.*[turns to leave, stepping over bodies as she does]*
> FIFTH DOCTOR: No, no, don't leave, not like this.
> TEGAN: I must! I'm sorry! Goodbye. *[Runs out of the warehouse in tears]* (Resurrection of the Daleks)

This is not a fairytale ending, but merely a human one. Tegan goes on to fight for Aboriginal rights in Australia (*Death of the Doctor*).

On the planet Sarn, American archaeologist Howard Foster is exploring with his stepdaughter Peri Brown. "The voluptuous Peri (Nicola Bryant) is regarded as a sex symbol among male fans more than any other companion" (Layton 110). Another critic, Kim Newman, smirks, "No 1980s guest character never mentions that Nicola Bryant's Peri is dressed like a porn star, though even giant earthworms and barbarian chiefs express an interest in having sex with her" (121). A college student, Peri wears short skirts and tight plunging tops that emphasize her hourglass figure, even after her bathing suit appearance. Turlough saves her from drowning, and she soon signs on as the new companion, an episode before the Fifth Doctor's regeneration.

Sixth Doctor (Colin Baker)

> SIXTH DOCTOR: Ahhh... a noble brow. Clear gaze. At least it will be given a few hours' sleep. A firm mouth. A face beaming with a vast intelligence. My dear child what on Earth are you complaining about? It's the most extraordinary improvement.
> PERI: *Improvement?!* On what?!
> SIXTH DOCTOR: My last incarnation... oh, I was never happy with that one. It had a sort of feckless "charm" which simply wasn't *me*
> PERI: What absolute rubbish! You were almost young, and you were sweet.
> SIXTH DOCTOR: "Sweet?!" *[scoff]* Effete! Sweet? Sweet? That says it all. No, this has been a timely change. *[Pauses, and stares into space]* Change? What change? There is no change... no time, no rhyme, no place for space, nothing! Nothing but the grinding engines of the universe, the crushing boredom of eternity! *[Collapses into a rack of coats and starts laughing hysterically, while Peri looks concerned]* (The Twin Dilemma)

Arrogant and dismissive, the Sixth Doctor was not terribly popular, though he had an eye-burning coat in primary colors. (This was selected to be in bad taste as possible and emphasize the Doctor's alienness.)

Half of his story is taken up with the *Trial of a Time Lord* sequence, which has him put on trial with the Valeyard as prosecutor. His crime? Interfering with other civilizations. This season-long story confusingly features episodes as retold and otherwise suspect testimony – i.e. some of the scenes shown have been tampered with and do not actually occur. This season, while offering clever plot twists, is problematic in more ways than its Doctor.

Companions

Peri is the Sixth Doctor's companion, but he attacks her while regenerating, in another moment that draws fans' ire:

> DOCTOR: How did you come by a name like that?
> PERI: It's the diminutive of my proper name, Perpugilliam.
> DOCTOR: Indeed. One morn, a peri at the gate of Eden stood disconsolate. Who wrote that?
> PERI: I haven't the faintest idea.
> DOCTOR: Of course you don't. You don't even know what a peri is, do you, Peri?
> PERI: No.
> DOCTOR: I'll tell you. A peri is a good and beautiful fairy in Persian mythology. The interesting thing is, before it became good, it was evil. And that's what you are. Thoroughly evil.
> PERI: Doctor, stop it!
> DOCTOR: No. No, not even a fairy. An alien spy, sent here to spy on me. Well, we all know the fate of alien spies.
> (The Doctor lunges at Peri and grabs her around the throat. She manages to grab the mirror from the console before he throws her to the floor, then she shows him his reflection. He lets her go, recoiling in tears.) (*The Twin Dilemma*)

"The Doctor's slapping Peri is excused because he's just regenerated, he has a newly-recharged alien mortality, he's not himself, it's a surprise for the audience, and so forth, but most fans reacted with revulsion – to them the Doctor just 'wouldn't do that'" (Muir 346). When he has recovered, he isn't much better. By rejecting the kindly Fifth Doctor, he shows a far nastier personality:

> DOCTOR: You may not believe this, but I have fully stabilized.

> PERI: Then I suggest you take a crash course in manners.
> DOCTOR: You seem to forget, Peri, I'm not only from another culture but another planet. I am, in your terms, an alien. I am therefore bound to different values and customs.
> PERI: Your former self was polite enough.
> DOCTOR: At such a cost. I was on the verge of becoming neurotic.
> PERI: We all have to repress our feelings from time to time. I suggest you get back into the habit.
> DOCTOR: And I would suggest, Peri, that you wait a little before criticizing my new persona. You may well find it isn't quite as disagreeable as you think.
> PERI: Well, I hope so.
> DOCTOR: Whatever else happens, I am the Doctor, whether you like it or not. (*The Twin Dilemma*)

By season end, the Doctor is shown sacrificing Peri to be killed (while this is revealed as a false scene that only happens in the tampered video, the chilling original disturbed viewers). *The Trial of a Time Lord* sequence ends with the Doctor's quick comment that Peri has not actually been sacrificed, but instead has wed the barbarian king of the planet. New companion Mel, who has met the Doctor offscreen, immediately shows up.

As one critic notes, "The nadir of the series' 80s slide into light-entertainment had to be the casting of Bonnie Langford as the preposterous Mel; a screeching annoyance whose one character trait was to make the Doctor drink carrot juice. She suddenly appeared in the middle of *The Trial of a Time Lord*, a season of linking narratives widely considered to be a nail in *Who*'s coffin. Langford's casting was another" (Martin). Melanie Bush was likely cast for her "star power" and made another frivolous, screaming companion. Producer John Nathan-Turner explains:

> I cast Bonnie, it was my idea, I thought she was right for the part. I also thought that bringing in someone who already had a name, as a companion, would help with publicity, to

refresh people's memory and to help with that. It was not a popular decision with many of the fans in Britain, but I think you have to keep that in perspective. Fans with a big 'f' who are members of the DWAS in Britain total 2,500 people, and over the years, for example when we were doing two episodes a week and getting ten million viewers, I think you have to keep the views of the fans in context. (*Doctor Who Interviews*)

She travels with the Sixth and Seventh Doctors for six multipart episodes. At last the young programmer and exercise nut from Sussex leaves the Seventh Doctor on Iceworld, to journey with the galactic confidence trickster Sabalom Glitz (*Dragonfire*).

Seventh Doctor (Sylvester McCoy)

At the start of the next season's *Time and the Rani*, the villainous Rani attacks the TARDIS and crashes it. The Doctor, near death, regenerates once again. His new incarnation suffers from amnesia, further confused by the Rani disguising herself as companion Mel. At last the Doctor works out his allies and enemies in time to save the day.

The Seventh Doctor transforms his coat from white to dark brown, just as his stories get darker and edgier. However, his question-mark pattered vest and question-mark cane make him seem more circus performer than conventional gentleman. "McCoy's outfit seemed like a childish conflation of past Doctors' dress: The Fifth's panama hat, the Second's check trousers, the First's spectator shoes, and so on" (Britton 50).

Upon regenerating, he tends to babble and invert expressions:

> DOCTOR: A bull in a barber shop. A navigational guidance system distorter. This would force any passing spaceship into landing here. Where are we, by the way?
> RANI: In your laboratory. On Lakertya. Doctor, are you sure you're well?
> DOCTOR: Of course. Fit as a trombone. (*Time and the Rani*)

He joins a circus and is mistaken for Merlin. His tendency to summersaults and theatrics only adds to this. Though a popular Doctor, he only lasted three seasons before the show's cancelation. He returns to be killed in the movie when he's gunned down in San Francisco then dies in surgery thanks to a doctor unfamiliar with his biology.

Companions

Dragonfire has Mel and teen punk Ace (Sophie Aldred) working together as a team. At the end, Mel persuades the Doctor to take Ace along on his adventures.

> MEL: Sorry. What about your chemistry A level, then?
> ACE: That's no good. I got suspended after I blew up the art room.
> MEL: You blew up the art room?
> ACE: It was only a small explosion. They couldn't understand how blowing up the art room was a creative act. (*Dragonfire*)

> ACE: I worked as a waitress in a fast food cafe. Day in, day out, same boring routine. Some boring life. It was all wrong. It didn't feel like me that was doing it at all. I felt like I'd fallen from another planet and landed in this strange girl's body, but it wasn't me at all. I was meant to be somewhere else. Each night I'd walk home and I'd look up at the stars through the gaps in the clouds, and I tried to imagine where I really came from. I dreamed that one day everything would come right. I'd be carried off back home, back to my real mum and dad. Then it actually happened and I ended up here. Ended up working as a waitress again, only this time I couldn't dream about going nowhere else. There wasn't nowhere else to go. (*Dragonfire*)

"I don't believe you've met my young friend Ace, an expert in calorification, incineration, carbonization, and inflammation," the Doctor says (*The Happiness Patrol*). With her bomber jacket and ponytail, she's best known for blowing things up with her beloved Nitro-9.

> SEVENTH DOCTOR: I don't suppose you've completely ignored my instructions and secretly prepared any Nitro-9, have you?
> ACE: What if I had?
> SEVENTH DOCTOR: And naturally, you wouldn't do anything so insanely dangerous as to carry it around with you, would you?
> ACE: Of course not. I'm a good girl and do what I'm told.
> SEVENTH DOCTOR: Excellent. Blow up that vehicle.

One of the most beloved companions, she lasted for two years before the show's 1989 cancelation. Her future is uncertain on the show, though she has more adventures in the audio series. Sarah Jane notes that by the year 2010, "There's a Dorothy something. She runs that company, A Charitable Earth. She's raised billions" (*Death of the Doctor*).

Eighth Doctor (Paul McGann)
The Eighth Doctor was created for the American television movie. He is a younger, handsomer Doctor and the first to kiss his companion (or anyone else) romantically. The Doctor finally experienced a first kiss onscreen, and the era of "no fooling around in the TARDIS" ended. If the movie had kicked off a revival of the show, this Doctor likely would have had romantic adventures, either with Doctor Grace or with new gals each week (or both!). As such, he appears less the quirky, asexual uncle and more a template for Doctors Ten and Eleven, who have relationships on the show.

> The Eighth Doctor arrives at Halloween, appropriately resuscitating in a morgue while the attendant is watching *Frankenstein*. The Eighth Doctor's outfit is full Victorian; he steals it from an actual Wild Bill Hickok costume, and discards the gunbelt and hat. (Thus the Third, Eighth, and Eleventh Doctors all steal their outfits from hospital lockers.) On the Eighth Doctor's audio and comic adventures, he keeps the same outfit, though it grows shabbier, and he finally replaces it with a similar cut but simpler materials. (Frankel, *What, Where, & How* 68-69)

While this is his only television appearance before 2013, he embarks on many audio adventures, with many companions. His reappearance in 2013, two decades older, suggests he has indeed been traveling through the galaxy.

In the Fiftieth Anniversary minisode "Night of the Doctor," a gunship crashes on the planet Karn. The sisterhood there warn the Doctor he's dying and offer him a controlled regeneration so he can end the Time War. He accepts.

Companions

The movie was "a co-American production, and that meant sex; not only McGann, with his angelic good looks, but Daphne Ashbrook with her large, well-displayed breasts – a second Peri, only with a medical degree" (Rose 46).

Though she's a doctor, she is haplessly responsible for Seven's death, and glamorous enough that she's difficult to take seriously. The Master and Doctor fight over her, as with many screaming companions:

> DOCTOR: How will you open the Eye now?
> MASTER: Grace, come here.
> DOCTOR: Unless I'm mistaken, in her present state of mind that won't work! Her eye's aren't human any more.
> MASTER: Watch.
> (The Master kisses Grace hard, sucking his presence out of her. Grace's eyes return to normal.)
> MASTER: See? Now they're human.
> DOCTOR: No! Grace, close your eyes!
> (The Master pushes Grace's face into the beam of light from the empty staff socket. She screams.)
> MASTER: Too late!

For about a decade, the Eighth Doctor was *the* Doctor – not on television, but in novels, comics, and Big Finish Audio Productions. After he traded Grace in, companions included:

- Samantha Jones
- Stacy Townsend
- Ssard

- C'rizz
- Fritz Kreiner
- Laura "Compassion" Tobin
- Anji Kappoor
- Beatrice "Trix" MacMillan
- Isabelle "Izzy" Sinclair
- Kroton
- Fey Truscott-Sade
- Destrii
- Samson Griffin
- Gemma Griffin
- Charlotte Pollard
- Lucie Miller

To fans' delight, he toasts the audio adventure companions in the minisode "Night of the Doctor," establishing them as canon: "Charley [Pollard], C'rizz, Lucie [Miller], Tamsin [Drew], Molly [O'Sullivan]" ("The Night of the Doctor").

War Doctor (John Hurt)

The Eighth Doctor realizes he must stop the Time War, but not as the Doctor, who only heals and aids. With the help of the Sisterhood, he regenerates into the War Doctor, an older man who is a rough, despairing realist. The Eleventh Doctor explains that this incarnation could not call himself the Doctor, adding, "The name you choose, it's like, it's like a promise you make. He's the one who broke the promise" ("The Name of the Doctor"). He stars in the Fiftieth Anniversary special "The Day of the Doctor" in 2013. In personality, he's motivated by desperation, but is critical and skeptical of Ten and Eleven: "Do you have to talk like children? What is it that makes you so ashamed of being a grown up?" he demands. He appears to be the only Doctor to have no living companion – only the voice of the Moment in his head.

It's unclear how long this incarnation lasts – it might be as little as a single day, or he might fight in the war for years (though on the same day as his death, Eleven notes that it's very early for him, suggesting a terribly brief lifespan). At the end of his one episode (excepting brief appearances in "The Name of the Doctor" and "The Night of the Doctor"), he notes that he's "wearing thin" and regenerates. Moffat comments that he preferred this lineup to having Eccleston be the War Doctor:

> ...do you know, I was always nervous of that one, because it doesn't fit with [1st episode of 2005's] Rose at all. Eccleston is a brand new Doctor in Rose, he's absolutely, definitely new. It couldn't have been is who pushed the button in the Time War, cos that's a new man, very explicitly, in that episode.
>
> Moffat also confessed he had a hard time "imagining it being Paul McGann's Doctor." In the end there was, to Moffat's mind, one best answer.
>
> So all of this led me to the idea that if you're going to sell to the Not-We audience a Doctor who essentially they haven't seen before, then you have a freer hand than saying it has to be one of the ones you've already had. And it was predicated in getting an enormous star to be able to do it. We got John Hurt, so that was cool! Think of the fuss it's created for us! (Roth, "Eccleston")

Ninth Doctor (Christopher Eccleston)

In 2005, Russell T Davies rebooted the show with the star of his miniseries *Second Coming*, Christopher Eccleston. " Russell T Davies knew that the Doctor had to come in swinging. That the show had to hook its audience from its opening moments, or it was in danger of fizzling, of being (like the eighth Doctor's brief tenure) a curiosity that didn't work" (Hambly, Kindle Locations 292-293).

The Doctor tells shopgirl Rose to run, they start running from the living mannequins, and the show is off and away. The rebooted show changes one major dynamic – the Doctor no longer serves the Time Lords, as he is the last, after a devastating Time War with the Daleks. His Doctor is angrier – less whimsical or flamboyant. In "Dalek," he confesses, "Ten million ships on fire. The entire Dalek race wiped out in one second…I watched it happen. I *made* it happen."

"Christopher Eccleston wore a crew cut and a black leather jacket and played the Doctor as the personification of John Lennon's iconic Working-Class Hero in the first season of Davies' revival" (DiPaolo 965-966). He may be the least colorful dresser of them all, fitting as he is so traumatized from the war. Not wanting to be typecast as the Doctor forever, Eccleston left after one year and did not return for the Fiftieth Anniversary. His character sacrifices himself to save Rose and defeat the Daleks at the end of their first year together.

Companions

Rose Tyler (Billie Piper) is the gateway character for new Who, a modern teen from London. She's smart, action-powered, and savvy. "She's positive, ambitious and full of conviction and confidence," said Piper. "She's ballsy and goes with her gut instinct. She's a good character to relate to or aspire to" (Gibson, Kindle Locations 357-363).

"She's a heroine," adds Eccleston. "She teaches him huge emotional lessons. They love each other. I think it's love at first sight, but it's not a conventional love affair, it's far more mysterious than that" (Gibson, Kindle Locations 357-363). While their relationship is ambiguous and barely defined with words, the Doctor appears to have romantic feelings for her, resolved in the Tenth Doctor's era.

The near-future scientist Adam Mitchell (Bruno Langley) travels with them briefly, but the Doctor returns him home, a zipper in his head, after he fails to follow the rules. Mickey Smith (Noel Clarke), Rose's boyfriend, stays on for more episodes, more successfully, despite the Doctor's rude comments and Rose's infatuation for the Doctor and occasionally Jack. They pick up Jack Harkness (John

Barrowman), 51st century bisexual Time Agent, on an adventure in World War II ("The Empty Child"/"The Doctor Dances") and he stays on through the end of the year, then returns for other adventures and finally gets a spinoff on *Torchwood*.

Tenth Doctor (David Tennant)

The Tenth Doctor has a blazing bright blue or brown or pinstripe suit, worn with bright red running shoes (or occasionally, a tux and running shoes). Tennant apparently begged producers to base his style on that of British celebrity chef Jaime Oliver. He also requested the comfortable trainers. Laura Mead writes in her teasingly titled essay, "David Tennant's Bum":

> I'd go so far as to argue that the advent of the Doctor as a new kind of sex symbol, the intelligent, pacifist hero, has led to a whole Christmas hamper of other similar characters speckled throughout popular culture, such as Benedict Cumberbatch's Sherlock Holmes. The watershed moment of the "Perfect Ten" Doctor has enabled fans to reappraise the hidden gems of genre television and the other rough diamonds including kindred roles such as Hugh Laurie's House and Nathan Fillion's Malcolm Reynolds. Even the more traditionally swashbuckling roles of Captains Jack Sparrow and the new Kirk now come complete with side orders of emotional angst and ennui. The alpha male, in all his bullet-spraying glory, is now frequently just a thin veneer over the more cerebral kind of hero women have grown to demand. (Kindle Locations 2943-2948).

Tennant, young, charming, and clever, raised *Doctor Who* fandom to previously unseen levels and became *the* Doctor for many fans.

The newly-regenerated Doctor battles the Sycorax to save earth. He loses a hand, but quickly regenerates it, as he's still filled with regeneration energy. Captain Jack finds the spare hand and uses it to track the Doctor. In "The Stolen Earth," a Dalek shoots the Doctor, who regenerates. However, he keeps the same form and channels the extra energy into the spare hand. When Donna touches it, it regenerates into a new Doctor, this one with part human DNA and many of her own mannerisms. This metacrisis Doctor, also sometimes called the Doctor-Donna, is also played by David Tennant. He stays with Rose in her alternate dimension, while the real Doctor continues to travel. While this incident counts as a regeneration (the Doctor is only allowed twelve), it does not add to the count of Doctors – David Tennant is Ten and Matt Smith is Eleven.

After a three-year run (series 2-4), then a bonus year of two hour specials, Tennant was ready to return to theater. Ten deliberately floods himself with radiation poisoning to save Donna's grandfather Wilfred Mott in "The End of Time." He returns for the Fiftieth Anniversary, but his adventures there are wiped from his mind.

Companions

While the Ninth Doctor finds Rose a comfort for his post-war trauma, the new "cool" Doctor who's "always alright" is a tougher emotional connection. Nonetheless, Rose is endlessly loyal to the Doctor:

> DOCTOR: Once the breach collapses, that's it. You will never be able to see her again. Your own mother!
> ROSE: I made my choice a long time ago, and I'm never going to leave you. So what can I do to help? ("Doomsday")

Nonetheless, she loses her grip and is nearly swept away until her alt-universe father grabs her and takes her to his world. She is condemned there forever, separated from the Doctor. She returns briefly in "Journey's End," and then is rewarded with a Doctor of her own. The Metacrisis Doctor, a part-human copy of Ten, can grow old with her in their own alt-world love story. Mickey, the third wheel, stays on Earth.

Freema Ageyman joins the cast the next year as Martha Jones. The actress notes of her character, "There are similarities with her and Rose. She's a feisty girl; she's a go-getter, she's not a wallflower" (Pool 852). Martha is the second medical doctor to become a companion and the first black woman. However, post-Rose, the Doctor treats Martha very badly indeed in her single year with him. He is hung up on Rose, more than past Doctors generally were for any companions. On New Earth, the Doctor takes Martha to the slums…he took Rose to the nicer section.

> MARTHA: You're taking me to the same planets that you took her?
> DOCTOR: What's wrong with that?
> MARTHA: Nothing. Just ever heard the word rebound?
> ("Gridlock")

She takes a job in a shop to support him in "Blink." Meanwhile he hesitates to make her his companion, taking her on "just one more trip" over and over. The Doctor only gives Martha a key in the seventh episode, after she's saved his life.

Worst is "Human Nature," in which she must scrub floors for arrogant white boys – for three months – because she lives in 1911. At episode end, Martha reveals her helpless crush for the Doctor, saying, "I've only just met him. It wasn't even that long ago. But he is everything. He's just everything to me and he doesn't even look at me, but I don't care, because I love him to bits. And I hope to God he won't remember me saying this." However, he remains oblivious. "Martha as John Smith's housemaid is not that different from Martha as the Doctor's companion. When we see Martha in a maid uniform, it's a visual amplification of her relationship to the Doctor, not a deviation from it" (Stoker, Kindle Locations 2559-2560).

At the end of her time with the Doctor, she walks the world for an entire year, preaching about the Doctor's goodness and inspiring the entire planet to believe in him. Meanwhile, the Master tortures her family. Afterwards, she decides to quit…because of her feelings for the Doctor:

MARTHA: Spent all these years training to be a doctor. Now I've got people to look after. They saw half the planet slaughtered and they're devastated. I can't leave them.
DOCTOR: Of course not. Thank you. Martha Jones, you saved the world.
MARTHA: Yes, I did. I spent a lot of time with you thinking I was second best, but you know what? I am good. You going to be all right?
DOCTOR: Always. Yeah.
MARTHA: Right then. Bye. (Martha leaves, then goes back inside.)Because the thing is, it's like my friend Vicky. She lived with this bloke, student housing, there were five of them all packed in, and this bloke was called Sean. And she loved him. She did. She completely adored him. Spent all day long talking about him.
DOCTOR: Is this going anywhere?
MARTHA: Yes. Because he never looked at her twice. I mean, he liked her, but that was it. And she wasted years pining after him. Years of her life. Because while he was around, she never looked at anyone else. And I told her, I always said to her, time and time again, I said, get out. So this is me, getting out. (She throws her mobile phone to him.) Keep that, because I'm not having you disappear. If that rings, when that rings, you'd better come running. Got it?

Martha returns for several episodes of *Torchwood*, in which she uses the alias Samantha Jones, an Eighth Doctor companion from the novels. She finally marries Mickey Smith as seen in "The End of Time."

Astrid Peth (Kylie Minogue) joins the Tenth Doctor for the 2007 special "Voyage of the Damned." A servant to wealthy spacegoers, she longs to see the world, but is killed just after the Doctor asks her to sign on permanently. Traveling with Donna and Martha together in "The Doctor's Daughter," a young woman is cloned from Ten and becomes his daughter Jenny. She appears to die, and Ten leaves her, but unknown to him, she revives and goes on adventures. She's played by Georgia Moffat, Peter Davison's daughter and eventually David Tennant's wife. Ten and Donna also meet River Song (Alex Kingston).

As series four arrives, Donna Noble (Catherine Tate), the Runaway Bride who was a single-episode companion a year previous, returns and establishes herself as very different from lovestruck Martha. Straight off, she proclaims that she has no interest in falling for the Doctor. The Doctor, as Tennant confesses, shows great relief when Donna "couldn't be less interested in him as anything other than a friend" ("Doctor Who Greatest Moments: The Companions").

> DONNA: You're not mating with me, sunshine!
> DOCTOR: A mate. I want a mate.
> DONNA: Well, just as well, because I'm not having any of that nonsense. I mean, you're just a long streak of nothing. You know, alien nothing.

She also refuses to follow orders:

> DONNA: What, and you're in charge?
> DOCTOR: TARDIS, Time Lord, yeah.
> DONNA: Donna, human, no. I don't need your permission. ("The Fires of Pompeii")

Further, she demands that he do more to interfere, rather than merely watching events. He has the power, therefore he should use it. "While the universe needs some kind of a savior, that savior needs to be questioned and challenged" (Deller 247)

> DONNA: Listen, I don't know what sort of kids you've been flying round with in outer space, but you're not telling me to shut up. That boy, how old is he, sixteen? And tomorrow he burns to death.
> DOCTOR: And that's my fault?
> DONNA: Right now, yes. ("The Fires of Pompeii")

When he refuses, she insists, "Just someone. Please. Not the whole town. Just save someone." After he does, the Doctor tells her, "You were right. Sometimes I need someone. Welcome aboard" ("The Fires of Pompeii").

She turns this lesson on herself in "Turn Left" – because

she can save the world, she must. "Perhaps the most noble human of all – and given her surname, that's not surprising – is Donna. It's Donna who continually challenges the Doctor's ethics, who's not afraid to tell him he's wrong, and who reminds him and the rest of the universe that humans are just as special as Time Lords" (Deller 245). The pair are also known for comedic babble:

> The Doctor and Donna are verbose to the point of euphoria and, save for Romana, no other Companion has ever matched his shrewdness. While some Classic Series companions can banter, it's often irresolute and subservient to his dexterity. Rose, River, and Martha are quick with rejoinders, but Donna outshines them all. (Burke 171)

Nonetheless, Donna suffers terribly. She says in "The Runaway Bride": "I missed my wedding, lost my job, and became a widow on the same day." Traveling in series four she loses her life on three separate occasions, and loses her husband and children. Finally, she joins with the Doctor to save everything as "the most important woman in the whole-wide universe" but loses that status along with all memory of the Doctor. He leaves her with only a lottery ticket.

Following this, the Doctor travels on solitary adventures for a year of four two-hour specials. Though he appears isolated and devastated by Donna's loss, he finds temporary companions in Victorian Jackson Lake (David Morrissey) who's been imprinted with the Doctor's personality and renowned thief Lady Christina de Souza (Michelle Ryan). Donna's grandfather, Wilf, is companion on Ten's last adventure, and Ten sacrifices himself to save Wilf, then travels space and time to bid each of his friends and companions goodbye.

Eleventh Doctor (Matt Smith)

> DOCTOR: Now all I've got to do is pass as an ordinary human being. Simple. What could possibly go wrong?
> AMY [OC]: Have you seen you?

DOCTOR: So you're just going to be snide. No helpful hints?
AMY: Hmm. Well, here's one. Bow tie, get rid.
DOCTOR: Bow ties are cool. Come on, Amy, I'm a normal bloke. Tell me what normal blokes do.
AMY [OC]: They watch telly, they play football. They go down the pub.
DOCTOR: I could do those things. I don't, but I could. ("The Lodger")

The Eleventh dresses as a nutty professor with tweed and bowtie, sporting "a Professor-from-*Gilligan's Island* allure" (Nussbaum 127). His old-fashioned wardrobe (and hopeless insistence that it's cool) contrasted with his youthful face gives him a strange, otherworldy quality. Matt Smith and Patrick Troughton (the Second Doctor) are both aping the "conventional 'boffin' of screen science fiction, with his untidy hair, bowtie, and baggy, unflattering attire" (Britton 43). He costumes with accessories – bow ties, a fez, a Stetson, and other ridiculous hats. The Doctor's bowtie is red if the episode takes place in the future, and blue if it's in the past.

He loves jammie dodgers and (in his first and final appearances) fish fingers with custard. He fits into society less well than some other Doctors, as he appears oblivious in many social situations, from clumsily attempting to live as a human in "The Lodger" to bursting from the cake at Rory's stag party and noting casually that he kissed Rory's fiancée.

Unlike many Doctors who might arguably live as briefly as a single year (though audio adventures and novels account for many more adventures), Eleven lives for several centuries and visibly ages before receiving a new set of regenerations. He is the first to have a wife and in-laws as a stable family, though his adventures with them take place out of order in producer Steven Moffat style.

Companions

The Moffat era began, not only with a long hiatus, but with new companions as well as a new Doctor in a fresh start quite atypical for the series. In "Meanwhile in the TARDIS," the short follow-up to Amy's seduction attempt in "Flesh and Stone," the Doctor explains why he has companions:

> DOCTOR: I'm 907. After a while, you just can't see it.
> AMY: See what?!
> DOCTOR: Everything – I look at a star, there's just a big ball of burning gas, and I know how it began and I know how it ends...and I was probably there both times. After a while, everything is just stuff. That's the problem; you make all of space and time your back yard, and what do you have? A back yard. But you; you can see it. And when you see it, I see it.

This emphasis that it's only an adventure if someone is watching it with fresh human eyes reflects on the viewers and emphasizes Amy's role as a viewer stand-in (even one who'd love a fling with the Doctor in this scene). Apparently the heart of the Doctor's travels is that human viewers are sharing them.

The regenerating Doctor lands on earth outside the home of Little Amelia Pond, a child who's been praying for someone to fix the crack in her wall, which spouts mysterious voices. After a night of silliness, the Doctor flits off for, as he thinks, just a moment, and accidentally returns when she's a nineteen-year-old kissogram girl (Karen Gillan). (The Doctor calls her The Girl Who Waited). Though Amy's quite sexualized, she calls the Doctor "Raggedy Man," her beloved imaginary childhood friend. Moffat explains:

> The basis of the relationship between the Doctor and the companion really is a magic man from space and a child... It's not boyfriend and girlfriend, it's not husband and wife, God knows, it's actually a magic man from space who can take you away, means you never have to go back to school, and a child. And that remains their relationship even when they're growed up a bit. - (qtd. in Hoskin 133)

They fight off the aliens and fly away together, though a final glimpse shows her waiting wedding dress. When the Doctor discovers midway through the year that she has fled her wedding, and is trying to seduce him, the rather horrified Doctor drags Amy's fiancé Rory Williams (Arthur Darvill) along, insisting they work out their problems. Rory is killed, sucked into the crack in time, but returns as an Auton in the fifth series finale. When his programming makes him shoot Amy, he then guards her for two millennia, earning the name the Centurion. Eleven seals the crack from outside the universe, but tells Amy that through concentrating, she can restore the real Rory, her parents, and even him. He returns for her wedding, and tells Amy and Rory goodbye; however, they insist on being the first companion married couple to stay with him.

They meet up with River Song (Alex Kingston) on occasion – this mysterious time traveler dies saving the Tenth Doctor in her future and knows the Doctor's name, suggesting she's his wife. In the Eleventh Doctor's time, she reveals she's in prison for murdering a good man, finally revealed to be the Doctor himself. Amy becomes pregnant, and her baby is stolen, but the Doctor finally discovers the baby, Melody Pond, will become River Song one day. River continues to travel with them on significant adventures, though she prefers not to be a permanent companion. Rory and Amy attempt to settle down without the Doctor but always return to him, until Rory is trapped in 1930s America in "The Angels Take Manhattan," and Amy decides to join him.

In Amy and Rory's final year with the Doctor, they visit the "Asylum of the Daleks" and meet Oswin Oswald (Jenna-Louise Coleman), a soufflé-making girl who saves the Doctor. In the Christmas special "The Snowmen," he meets governess Clara Oswin Oswald, a copy of this first character and "impossible girl."

He tracks down her modern incarnation, Clara Oswald, in 2013 London. She becomes his companion as he struggles to solve the mystery. At last, after a quick eight episodes, the Great Intelligence enters the Doctor's self and tries to destroy him throughout time and space. Clara follows and saves all the incarnations of the Doctor in every moment, then Eleven succeeds in pulling her to safety. Clara's charges (she's a nanny) and later students from Coal Hill Elementary join them on several adventures. Moffat notes:

> In a way, *Doctor Who* is almost more the story of the companion. It's her take on the Doctor. It's the adventure that she goes on with the Doctor. That's the story that we tell. The companion changes more than the Doctor ever does. So, what Jenna, in particular, brings is that she has a speed and wit and an unimpressed quality that makes the Doctor dance a bit harder, I suppose. He works a bit harder with Clara. Obviously, she's secretly devoted to him, but she's a little bit harder to impress. She's tough, she's fast and she's hard to impress, which is exactly the way the Doctor, generally speaking, doesn't like them, but of course, he's absolutely devoted to Clara. That's very much driven by Jenna's particular style, which is very, very fast and snappy. She's a beautiful girl, but there's a real sense of toughness, and she's someone who can be a real adversary, if she wants to be. (Radish)

Twelfth Doctor (Peter Capaldi)

Peter Capaldi takes the Doctor from his youngest actor to one of the oldest. As such, he must spend a great deal of effort winning over young fans. He is quirky, often snapping at or dismissing Clara, but following this with statements of heartbreaking sweetness and utter trust. He wears simple, stark black with dramatic red lining in his coat. Twelve returns to the more asexual uncle or grandfather to his companion. While Clara introduces Eleven as her boyfriend to her family (and by showing up nude, he makes the worst possible impression), Twelve hints that he wants to size up Clara's love interest as a substitute father…or even check the young man's future to discover his prospects.

Clara is Twelve's companion, joined occasionally by her boyfriend Danny Pink and her students, though she is set to leave at the Christmas Special.

Story Arcs

Repeated Arc Words

Series One

The words "bad wolf" appear in dialogue from the Moxx of Balhoon in "The End Of The World," mentioned by Gwyneth in "The Unquiet Dead," as graffiti painted on the TARDIS in "Aliens Of London"/"World War Three," as Henry van Statten's codename in "Dalek," as a TV channel in "The Long Game," scrawled on a poster in "Father's Day," the name of the bomb (in German) in "The Empty Child"/"The Doctor Dances," and the name of nuclear power station (in Welsh) in "Boom Town." Darlig Ulv Stranden, Bad Wolf Bay in Norway, is Rose's alt-world weak point between worlds, where she says two goodbyes to the Doctor.

Series Two

The Torchwood Institute is casually mentioned in "Bad Wolf," "School Reunion," "Rise of the Cybermen," "The Idiot's Lantern," "Love & Monsters," and "Fear Her." The institute creates and fires the weapon of "The Christmas Invasion." It's the agency responsible for the mission to the black hole in "The Impossible Planet"/"The Satan Pit," and is created by Queen Victoria in "Tooth and Claw," before featuring in the two part finale, then recreated as Torchwood Three on the spinoff television show.

Series Three
In 2006's "Love & Monsters," a newspaper headline reads "Saxon Leads Polls with 64 Percent" In "The Runaway Bride," the British military is following Saxon's orders, while his name appears on a news broadcast and election poster in "Smith and Jones." (The poster also appears in the *Torchwood* episode "Captain Jack Harkness.") Agents of Mr. Saxon give Francine Jones cryptic warnings in "The Lazarus Experiment" and "42." Meanwhile, the concept of the Doctor turning human with his Time Lord essence in a watch appears in "Human Nature"/"The Family of Blood." With the prophecy of the Face of Boe: "You Are Not Alone," "the stage is set for the three-part finale.

Series Four
In the next year, the planets of the adipose and the Pyroviles vanish. In "Midnight," Dee Dee mentions her paper on the lost moon of Poosh. The honeybees are disappearing. The Master mentions the Medusa Cascade. With prophecies such as "There's something on your back" to Donna and "She is coming," referencing Rose Tyler's momentary cameos, the fourth series is exploding with arc references.

In the 2009 specials, "He will knock four times" become the arc words, offered by a human seer in "Planet of the Dead." She adds: "[Gallifrey] is returning. It is returning through the dark, and then Doctor... oh but then... he will knock four times." Characters in "Planet of the Ood" and "The Wedding of Sarah Jane Smith" mention the Doctor's upcoming fate. In "The Waters of Mars," the Doctor thunders that an alien adversary won't get to knock more than three times and tries to alter a fixed point, but fails. When "The End of Time" finally comes, the Master's four-beat sound in his head appears to be the four knocks. However, the Doctor survives the Time Lord invasion and saves the day, only to hear Wilfred knocking to be let out. Four times. The Doctor sacrifices himself, then bids goodbye to all the Davies-era companions, along with the Davies era itself, bookending the show.

Series Five

For the fifth series, the crack on Amy's wall is the "arc image," appearing in every episode. The issues of Amy and Rory's abandoned wedding, then her forgetting Rory get a nod in each episode. River Song also mentions that the Pandorica adventure is coming soon as she leaves in "Flesh and Stone." The two-part finale acts as a sequel to every single series five episode: Vincent van Gogh ("Vincent and the Doctor") has a premonition, which he paints and delivers to Winston Churchill ("Victory of the Daleks"), who sends it to Liz Ten's art gallery ("The Beast Below"), and calls River Song ("The Time of Angels"), who finally delivers it. Rory, lost in "Cold Blood," reappears, as does Young Amelia from "The Eleventh Hour" and finally Amy and Rory's wedding takes place.

Combining the plot of the Pandorica with the following year's Silence, Prisoner Zero tells the Doctor that "The universe is cracked. The Pandorica will open. Silence will fall" in "The Eleventh Hour." The Silence's ship (seen in "The Lodger") also returns the following year.

There is a great deal of waiting, not just for Amy, who waits half her life for the Doctor, but also for Rory, revived as a Roman, for centuries-old Liz Ten, and for River in prison.

The Doctor's enemies in the Series Five finale episode include just about every new series prosthetic alien (as old series ones and more complex creatures like the Atraxi would have required more work): Judoon ("Smith and Jones"), Hoix ("Love & Monsters"), Silurians ("The Hungry Earth"), Robo-forms ("The Christmas Invasion"), Uvodni (*The Sarah Jane Adventures*: "Warriors of Kudlak"), and Blowfish (*Torchwood*: "Kiss Kiss Bang Bang"), as well as Daleks, Cybermen, and Sontarans. *Doctor Who Confidential* notes that this many different monsters had never before been seen side by side. River describes the ships overhead as Daleks, Cybermen,

Sontarans, Terileptils ("The Visitation"), Slitheen ("Aliens of London"), Nestene ("Rose"), Drahvin ("Galaxy Four"), Sycorax ("The Christmas Invasion"), Zygons ("Terror of the Zygons"), Atraxi ("The Eleventh Hour"), Draconians ("Frontier in Space"), and even Chelonians (from the novel *The Highest Science*), and Haemo-Goths (from the novel *The Forgotten Army*).

Series Six
Series Six begins with the Doctor's death in "The Impossible Astronaut." *Who* writer Gareth Roberts notes a theme of "death and lingering darkness" through the sixth series ("Open All Hours"). As he adds, "Time is closing in on him and he can't put off going to Lake Silencio and his doom" ("An Interview with Gareth Roberts"). The phrase "silence will fall" mirrors the inevitable death, though ironically, silence will only fall if the Doctor lives. Through the many revelations about River Song as they fall in love in the wrong order, the Doctor learns of his upcoming death and tries to escape the inevitable. In the process, the Doctor spends two hundred years seeing the universe and waving to his friends from the history books. As the Doctor puts it:

> Been knocking about. A bit of a farewell tour. Things to do, people to see. There's always more. I could invent a new color, save the Dodo, join the Beatles...For me, it never stops. Liz the First is still waiting in a glade to elope with me. I could help Rose Tyler with her homework. I could go on all of Jack's stag parties in one night. ("The Wedding of River Song")

As his arc ends in "Night Terrors," "Closing Time," and "The Wedding of River Song," creepy children sing foreboding nursery rhymes, heralding the Doctor's fate. In this series, the mysterious face looking at Amy and the revelation that she's a type of ganger are tied to River's birth, of course. There are more reunions: "A Good Man Goes to War" unites the pirates, Danny Boy, Dorium, Madame

Vastra, Jenny, Strax, and all the Doctor's allies. Rory even dresses as a Roman. On the opposite side are clerics, Cybermen, headless monks, and endless soldiers.

"The Wedding of River Song" features Churchill and Dickens in the out-of-time universe, along with Daleks, pterodactyls ("Everything Changes"), Cleopatra ("The Pandorica Opens"), the Teselecta ("Let's Kill Hitler"), Silurians ("Cold Blood"), and Dorium ("A Good Man Goes to War"). Amy sketches her past adventures: Daleks, Silurians, vampires, pirates, and Weeping Angels. River also recruits everyone in the universe to help, saying,

> "The sky is full of a million, million voices saying yes, of course we'll help. You've touched so many lives, saved so many people. Did you think when your time came, you'd really have to do more than just ask? You've decided that the universe is better off without you, but the universe doesn't agree."

This episode bookends events of all the River Song episodes, especially "Forest of the Dead," "The Impossible Astronaut," and "A Good Man Goes to War," while setting up Trenzalore and the question that will provide the next year's arc.

Series Seven
Series Seven guides viewers through Rory and Amy's balancing a normal life with their Doctor adventures, then Clara's short arc as the Eleventh Doctor's Impossible Girl. The latter offers her favorite expressions and talismans: soufflés, "Run, you clever boy and remember," and her parents' special leaf, along with her jobs as governess and protector. She also reads Amelia Pond's book. Trenzalore and the adventures of Vastra's Victorian team continue through the series, all culminating in "The Name of the Doctor."

Series Eight
Peter Capaldi and Clara trade the phrase "Do as you're told,"

emphasizing the power dynamic between them, as well as her comforting him with this expression when he was a child ("Listen"). This episode and many others explore the mix of duty and fear behind choosing to be a soldier, from the Doctor himself to Danny Pink to Gretchen in "Into the Dalek" and even the mummy on the Orient Express. This culminates as Danny and the Brigadier both choose their final fates as soldiers defending the living on earth.

Mostly the arc character is Missy, a mysterious figure welcoming many characters into "Paradise" when they die. She watches and judges the Doctor's activities, and is finally revealed as the woman who brought Clara the Doctor in "The Bells of Saint John" and "Deep Breath" as well as the Master, scheming to conquer earth by using the dead.

Untangling Moffat's Plots

Russell T. Davies' plot arcs (shown above) aren't overly complex – Torchwood or "Mr. Saxon" gains power over a season, then unleashes it in the finale. But Moffat's plots, generally involving time travel, paradoxes, and multiple years of unraveling, can be far more complex. So here they are, unspooled and unraveled for the viewers' understanding.

The Crack in Time

- Amy Pond enters the series praying for someone to come fix the crack in her wall, since she can hear voices through it. It's later revealed that the crack has also swallowed her parents and all memory of them. Upon examining it, the Eleventh Doctor calls the crack "two parts of space and time that should never have touched, pressed together" and ("The Eleventh Hour") "cracks in the skin of the universe." ("The Pandorica Opens"). While the Doctor closes this crack, others appear during his and Amy's other adventures.
- He returns just before Amy's wedding, drawn to the exact moment because of its complication in time. On 26 June 2010, the night before Amy's wedding, she runs off with the Doctor. They return a few minutes later to snatch up Rory and take him along.
- The crack erases many events including Rory himself when he falls into it. The Doctor guesses that the cracks had erased memorable events such as the CyberKing's invasion of Victorian London and the 2009 Dalek invasion of Earth. The ducks from a duck pond in Leadworth vanish in another symptom ("Flesh and Stone")
- In "Cold Blood," the Doctor retrives a fragment of his TARDIS from a crack, suggesting it's the cause.
- He hurls a shipful of Weeping Angels into the crack to close it temporarily ("Flesh and Stone").

- On 26 June 2010, the Silence make the TARDIS materialize outside Amy's house and River, flying it back to the Doctor, loses control. The TARDIS explodes, shattering all of space and time. The TARDIS saves the universe by placing it in a time loop, while the explosion warms the earth in place of the sun. The Doctor salvages a few particles of the original universe from the perfect preservation of the Pandorica and uses them to restart the universe.

- While repairing the universe, the Doctor is left outside it. He travels backwards in time through his adventures with Amy and tells her she must remember him. The Doctor realizes that Amy's lifetime proximity to the crack has given her unusual perception and influence – if she remembers her parents, Rory, and the Doctor himself, all will come back...they do, just in time for the wedding.

- On the Minotaur's prison ship, the crack reappears inside the room of the Doctor's worst fear, suggesting the cracks have not been completely repaired ("The God Complex").

- Startlingly, the crack reappears years later in "The Time of the Doctor," creating a bookend on the series:

> CLARA: What's wrong? It's only a crack in the wall.
> OCTOR: I knew. I always knew it wasn't over.
> CLARA: What is it?
> DOCTOR: A split in the skin of reality.
> (As he touches it, he is remembers other times the crack was there.)
> DOCTOR: A tiny sliver of the 26th of June, 2010. The day the universe blew up.
> CLARA: Missed that.
> DOCTOR: I rebooted it, put it all back together.
> CLARA: That's good.
> DOCTOR: Well, it was my TARDIS that blew it up in the first place. I felt a degree of responsibility. But the scar tissue remains. A structural weakness in the whole universe. Whoa! And someone's trying

to get through it from outside our universe, from somewhere else. Of course. Of course. It makes sense.
CLARA: It does?
DOCTOR: Yes. If you were trying to break through a wall, you'd choose the weakest spot. If you were trying to break into this universe, you'd choose this crack, because. No. If you were trying to break back into this universe.

TASHA LEM: The Kovarian Chapter broke away. They travelled back along your timeline and tried to prevent you ever reaching Trenzalore.
DOCTOR: So that's who blew up my TARDIS. I thought I'd left the bath running.
TASHA: They blew up your time capsule, created the very cracks in the universe through which the Time Lords are now calling.
DOCTOR: The destiny trap. You can't change history if you're part of it.

Madam Kovarian is responsible for destroying the TARDIS and causing the crack in "The Pandorica Opens"/"The Big Bang," as well as the re-engineering of River Song. Ironically, these acts *lead* to the events they were trying to prevent ("The Time of the Doctor").

The Time Lords reach through the crack to give the Doctor more regenerations and save him from his final battle. Thus the crack closes and the Silence achieve their goal. In a further bookend on the series, the Doctor imagines young and grown Amelia Pond coming to bid him goodbye. He sheds his raggedy man clothes and bowtie, eats fish fingers and custard, and otherwise bids goodbye to himself as Eleven.

The Pandorica and Rory the Roman

As a child, Amy adores anything to do with Rome, especially handsome centurions. Amy notes that the

81

Romans were "My favorite topic at school. Invasion of the hot Italians. Yeah, I did get marked down for the title." She also has a beloved book of mythology on Pandora's Box, with the world's most dangerous secrets within.

►◄ On their travels, Rory is killed, sucked into the crack. Thus Amy loses all memory of him. The Doctor keeps her engagement ring for her.

►◄ Vincent has a vision and paints a message for the Doctor. The news goes from him to Churchill to River Song, who steals the painting from Liz Ten, as all of series fives's heroes unite to save the Doctor ("The Pandorica Opens"). River summons the Doctor to ancient Britain and warns him the Pandorica, beneath Stonehenge, is opening.

> AMY: The Pandorica? What is it?
> RIVER: A box, a cage, a prison. It was built to contain the most feared thing in all the universe.
> DOCTOR: And it's a fairy tale, a legend. It can't be real.
> RIVER: If it is real, it's here and it's opening, and it's got something to do with your TARDIS exploding. Hidden, obviously. Buried for centuries. You won't find it on a map.
> DOCTOR: No, but if you buried the most dangerous thing in the universe, you'd want to remember where you put it.

►◄ All the villains of the show have constructed a trap from Amy's memories, from her favorite fictional characters. The Romans are artificial Nestene duplicates and begin to attack. The Doctor's enemies shut him in the Pandorica and Rory succumbs to his programming for a moment and kills Amy. The TARDIS crashes with River flying it, and all the universe is lost except for a brief loop of time, preserved by the TARDIS itself ("The Pandorica Opens").

DOCTOR: You lot, working together. An alliance.
How is that possible?
WHITE: The cracks in the skin of the universe.
STARK: All reality is threatened.
CYBERLEADER: All universes will be deleted.
DOCTOR: What? And you've come to me for help?
STARK: No. We will save the universe from you!
DOCTOR: From me?
CYBERLEADER: All projections correlate. All
evidence concurs. The Doctor will destroy the
universe.
DOCTOR: No, no, no. You've got it wrong.
CYBERLEADER: The Pandorica was constructed
to ensure the safety of the Alliance.
WHITE: A scenario was devised from the
memories of your companion.
STARK: A trap the Doctor could not resist.
WHITE: The cracks in time are the work of the
Doctor. It is confirmed.

Though the Doctor protests that it is the TARDIS not him – in fact he is the only one who can stop it – his enemies shut him in the Pandorica. Rory sits alone in ancient Rome with Amy's corpse.

The Doctor pops in from thin air, wearing a fez and carrying a mop. He tells Rory, "Rory! Listen, she's not dead. Well, she is dead, but it's not the end of the world. Well, it is the end of the world. Actually, it's the end of the universe. Oh, no. Hang on." The Doctor convinces Rory he can act human enough to save Amy through his love for her, and they put her in the Pandorica. The Doctor adds, "The Pandorica can stasis-lock her that way. Now, all it needs is a scan of her living DNA and it'll restore her." He takes River's vortex manipulator from her abandoned bag, but auton-Rory chooses to guard Amy in the Pandorica for two millennia. In the future, the Doctor enlists little Amelia and releases Amy from the Pandorica only to find auton-Rory waiting. They find a dying Doctor from twelve minutes in the future, though it turns out he faked his death.

> RIVER: The TARDIS is still burning. It's exploding at every point in history. If you threw the Pandorica into the explosion, right into the heart of the fire.
> AMY: Then what?
> RIVER: Then let there be light. The light from the Pandorica would explode everywhere at once, just like he said.
> AMY: That would work? That would bring everything back?
> RIVER: A restoration field powered by an exploding TARDIS, happening at every moment in history. Oh, that's brilliant. It might even work. He's wired the vortex manipulator to the rest of the box.
> AMY: Why?
> RIVER: So he can take it with him. He's going to fly the Pandorica into the heart of the explosion. ("The Big Bang")

►◄ The Doctor restarts the universe from outside it, but Amy's memories bring him back in the middle of the wedding. Meanwhile Amy's memories also bring back her parents and human-Rory, though he remembers his time as a Roman.

►◄ Amy and Rory are caught roleplaying as policewoman and centurion in "A Christmas Carol."

►◄ Amy proudly describes Rory to baby Melody as the Centurion in "A Good Man Goes to War," and Rory wears the outfit to reinforce his reputation.

►◄ Several times, Eleven calls Rory "Centurion," usually while requesting "permission to hug" Amy.

River Song/Melody Pond

River Song first appears to the Tenth Doctor during his adventures with Donna in "Silence in the Library"/ "Forest of the Dead." To his shock, she knows his name (something he would only tell one person – presumably his wife). She dies saving him, though he manages to preserve her in the Library's computers. She appears again in "The Time of the Angels"/"Flesh and Stone," this time a convict rather than an archeologist, condemned to prison for murdering someone. She aids the Doctor with the Pandorica, and appears outside Rory and Amy's wedding, when he accidentally proposes to her. She gives him their first kiss in "Day of the Moon." However, only in "A Good Man Goes to War" does she drop the coy hints and tell him who she is: Melody Pond. Melody's childhood with Amy and Rory, and her transformation into River Song all appear in "Let's Kill Hitler," and her life is laid out in order from her point of view below. The Tesselecta (tiny people hiding in a human-sized robot) try to execute her for murdering the Doctor, but the Doctor gets her a reprieve.

The cap on "The Impossible Astronaut" and the Doctor's forthcoming death appears in "The Wedding of River Song" – she is the mysterious figure who murdered the Doctor in front of his friends. By trying to change this moment, she collapses the timestream so that all moments happen at once. The Doctor convinces her to undo it, but dodges death himself in a Tesselecta body. He visits his new wife River in prison for outings. With all secrets out, Eleven, Amy, Rory, and River interact as a family until Amy and Rory are lost in the past. River then presumably sacrifices herself saving the Doctor in his past and bids the Doctor goodbye as a data ghost in "The Name of the Doctor." Events from her perspective are notably different:

- Melody Pond is born in the 52nd century on Demon's Run but taken to 20th century earth when a newborn to be raised to kill the Doctor.
- Melody grows up in a Florida orphanage, raised by the Silence. River later reveals that the Silence put her in a spacesuit to give her some independence.

> RIVER: It's an exoskeleton. Basically, life support.
> There's about twenty different kinds of alien tech in
> here.
> DOCTOR: Who was she? Why put her in here?
> RIVER: You put this on, you don't even need to
> eat. The suit processes sunlight directly. It's got
> built in weaponry, and a communications system
> that can hack into anything. ("Day of the Moon")

- As a terrified child in July 1969, she wanders through Florida calling for help and encounters her mother, Amy Pond. Her mother almost kills her, though she apologizes later ("Day of the Moon"). Melody likely recognizes her from a photo.
- Six months later in New York, Melody grows ill and regenerates into a frightened toddler. She somehow travels thirty years into the future (or more likely lives those thirty years then regenerates into a young girl again), travels to Leadworth, and becomes a best friend to Amy and Rory when they're seven or a bit older. She displays an obsession with the Doctor ("Let's Kill Hitler").
- As a teenager, she alerts Amy that Rory is in love with her.
- A 21-year-old Amy, engaged to Rory, runs away with the Doctor and then returns and weds Rory the next day (earth time, admittedly with some rewriting of history) ("The Big Bang"). Melody is invited but deliberately skips her parents' wedding. (An older version of her also skips it but meets the Doctor outside. He proposes to her inadvertently and she accepts.)
- Melody, now 21 like her friends, drives up meets the Doctor, and hijacks him to kill Hitler. There she asks the Doctor to marry her and when shot regenerates into the current incarnation of River Song. She kisses the Doctor for the first time, poisoning him with lipstick ("Let's Kill Hitler"). Kovarian has

86

brainwashed her into a violent obsession with her idol.

►◄ The TARDIS teaches Melody to drive it. Amy reveals that Melody is going to be River Song, the Doctor's beloved. The Doctor says that he loves her. Touched, she kisses the Doctor for the second time and transfers all her regeneration energy to him.

> RORY: Doctor, River was brainwashed to kill you, right?
> DOCTOR: Well, she did kill me, and then she used her remaining lives to bring me back. As first dates go, I'd say that was mixed signals. ("Let's Kill Hitler")

►◄ The Doctor takes River to the "best hospital in the universe" to recover and leaves her a journal. After recuperating, she enters the Luna University in 5123. She decides to study archeology.

►◄ On the day she completes her degree, Kovarian and the Silence come for her:

> RIVER: You know about the Doctor?
> KOVARIAN: So very well. Oh, don't try and remember me. We've been far too thorough with your dear little head.
> (Two Silence creep up behind River.)
> RIVER: Oh! What are they? What are those things?
> KOVARIAN: Your owners.
> RIVER: My what?
> KOVARIAN: So, they made you a Doctor today, did they? Doctor River Song. How clever you are. You understand what this is, don't you?
> RIVER: According to some accounts, it's the day the Doctor dies.
> KOVARIAN: By Silencio Lake, on the Plain of Sighs, an Impossible Astronaut will rise from the deep and strike the Time Lord dead. ("Closing Time")

➡ By refusing to shoot the Doctor, she plunges them into an alternate reality where all of time is happening at once and "silence falls." In the alternate reality, brainwashed and uncertain who she is, she weds the Doctor and he forgives her for the murder. However, when they're transported back to the instant on Silencio Lake, the Doctor fakes his death ("The Wedding of River Song").

➡ She is sentenced to twelve thousand consecutive life sentences in the Stormcage Containment Facility in the 52nd century (by 5145). She serves the sentence to make the Silence believe her husband is dead, but starting with her first night, escapes often to spend nights with her husband, then returns to her cell.

➡ On her first night in prison, The Doctor arrives in a white tux to take her to Calderon Beta to show her the sky on the starriest night in the entire universe. He tells her their diary rules and explains how their backwards life will fit together. Unknown to her, two other Rivers pass through the TARDIS that night, one on her final date with her husband. ("First Night," "Last Night")

> The readthrough script for [The Impossible Astronaut] had minimal changes before issue as shooting script. The main alteration was the ultimately deleted scene at Stormcage where the governor remonstrated with River Song over her previous 15 escapes under his predecessor, "Oh, it was never fifteen – unless you're counting holidays and hair appointments..." said River as she opened a cupboard on the cell wall and pulled out an impossibly long clothes rail of dresses commenting, "Don't mind my wardrobe. Teensy bit bigger on the inside!" (Anders)

➡ The Doctor tells River his name at some point. River says only, "I made him" and "It took a while" ("The

Name of the Doctor"). She also meets Kate, judging by a photo of them in "The Day of the Doctor."

➤ River is invited to Silencio Lake. She has a family picnic then sees the Impossible Astronaut kill the Doctor. She pretends not to know who it is ("The Impossible Astronaut").

➤ River receives the Doctor's call for help to come to Demon's Run. She arrives late, but confesses to Amy and Rory that events had to happen this way for their kidnapped daughter to grow into her ("A Good Man Goes to War").

➤ Exploring the 1930s, River finds Rory, who's been dragged back in time by the weeping angels, and summons the Doctor. However, after saving Rory and returning to the present, she and the Doctor are horrified when an angel snatches him into the past once more, to a time too muddled for the Doctor to reach. Amy bids them both farewell, and joins Rory there. River reaches Amy to ask her to write the Doctor a final goodbye.

➤ River journeys to the Pandorica, masquerading as Cleopatra. Rory meets her for his first time. After, she stops outside her parents' wedding and lends them her journal. She smilingly accepts the Doctor's proposal.

➤ In "Time of the Angels"/"Flesh and Stone," she's recruited as an advisor for the clergy and she promises them the equivalent of an army (the Doctor). For this, they take her temporarily from the prison. It's likely that she earns a pardon for her actions here, saving the universe from an invasion of angels, though the bishop and his followers all perish. She mentions she's not yet a professor of archeology. Amy and the Eleventh Doctor meet her; she pretends not to know their significance.

THE CATCHUP GUIDE TO DOCTOR WHO

- After this she travels to see future Amy and Rory and tells them the Doctor is alive ("The Wedding of River Song").
- The Doctor dresses in a black tux and River finally wears the green dress he suggested for their first date. They go to see the Singing Towers of Darillium. She accidentally bumps into the Doctor on his first night out with her ("First Night," "Last Night"). The Doctor gives her his sonic screwdriver.
- The Doctor meets her for his first time in The Library, the youngest she's ever seen him. She sacrifices herself for the Doctor and dies in the 51st century on the Library planet, but the Doctor saves her consciousness digitally to the Library's computer, granting her a form of theoretical immortality.
- River reappears in "The Name of the Doctor." She introduces herself to Clara and saves the Doctor's companions by using his name to open the tomb. says goodbye to the Doctor, adding that her data ghost is degrading.

> DOCTOR: You are always here to me. And I always listen, and I can always see you.
> RIVER: Then why didn't you speak to me?
> DOCTOR: Because I thought it would hurt too much.
> RIVER: I believe I could have coped.
> DOCTOR: No, I thought it would hurt me. And I was right.
> (The Doctor kisses River.)
> DOCTOR: Since nobody else in this room can see you, God knows how that looked. There is a time to live and a time to sleep. You are an echo, River. Like Clara. Like all of us, in the end. My fault, I know, but you should've faded by now.
> RIVER: It's hard to leave when you haven't said goodbye.
> DOCTOR: Then tell me, because I don't know. How do I say it?
> RIVER: There's only one way I'd accept. If you ever loved me, say it like you're going to come

back.
DOCTOR: Well, then. See you around, Professor River Song.
RIVER: Till the next time, Doctor.
DOCTOR: Don't wait up.
RIVER: Oh, there's one more thing.
DOCTOR: Isn't there always?
RIVER: I was mentally linked with Clara. If she's really dead, then how can I still be here?
DOCTOR: Okay, how?
RIVER: Spoilers. Goodbye, sweetie.

Despite her second death, her last words suggest she hasn't quite gone.

> Moving on to River Song, Moffat says he's "not quite sure" yet if she'll be back: "I mean we can see her again because everything's out of sequence and clearly the implication is that she's met more than two Doctors. But the question is whether or not we should revisit her. It'll now be story-driven. If we've got an idea that she fits into perfectly then there's no reason why we can't do it, but I quite liked where we got to at the end of 'The Name of the Doctor,' with him saying goodbye to her. So we'll see." ("Moffat talks Valeyard")

►◄ Tasha Lem, the Mother Superious and Head of the Church of the Papal Mainframe, appears in the following episode, "The Time of the Doctor." Many fans believe she is River Song returned. She provides the voiceover, something seen from River in "The Forest of the Dead." Upon greeting him, she begins flirting and invites him into her bedroom.

TASHA: Hey, babes.
DOCTOR: Loving the frock.
TASHA: Is that a new body? Give us a twirl.
DOCTOR: Tash, this old thing? Please, I've been rocking it for centuries.
TASHA: Nice though. Tight.
CLARA: So, er, hello. Also here.
…

DOCTOR: [The Time Lords are] asking for my help!
TASHA: And if you give it, war will be the consequence. I
will not let that happen, at any cost. Speak your name and
this world will burn.
DOCTOR: No, this planet is protected.
...
DOCTOR: You never could resist a row.
TASHA: Kiss me when I ask.
DOCTOR: Well, you'd better ask nicely.
TASHA: In your dreams.
DOCTOR: Right, get us back to the TARDIS. Can you do
that?
TASHA: Yeah, but quickly, the Dalek inside me is waking.
DOCTOR: Fight it.
TASHA: I can't.
DOCTOR: Listen to me. You have been fighting the
psychopath inside you all your life. Shut up and win. That is
an order, Tasha Lem.
TASHA: The forcefield will hold for a while, but it will decay,
and there are breaches already.
DOCTOR: Then this isn't a siege any more, it's a war. It's
all up to you now. Fight the Daleks, inside and out. You can
do it, I know you can.
TASHA: Oh, I see. You've got your TARDIS back, haven't
you? Time to fly away.
DOCTOR: Tasha, please. Please. Thank you.
TASHA: None of this was for you, you fatuous egotist. It
was for the peace. Fly away, Doctor!
...
TASHA: Flying the TARDIS was always easy. It was flying
the Doctor I never quite mastered.

While she might be a new character, the likelihood is that
she's River (from the preceding arc) or the Mistress (from
the following arc). Clues in the dialogue are ambiguous:
Both River and the Mistress have been perpetually
fighting their inner psychopaths and enjoy battling and
flirting with the Doctor. Both have flown the TARDIS
(though River has spent more time flying the *Doctor's*
TARDIS). The Mistress has not seen Eleven's body while
River certainly has. However, Twelve is shocked when
reencountering the Mistress, and not inclined to flirt back
when she kisses him and makes advances. A previous

friendly relationship with her would suggest many missed adventures (possible of course) but also events that are seriously out of order (also possible). Tasha is determined to prevent a Time War (more likely for River than the Master) and the Doctor mentions his life with River, another wink to the audience.

Whichever, the case, Tasha Lem dies in the episode, screaming the Doctor's name, and is transformed into one of the Daleks. She will continue the fight from within the Dalek Empire, in a fascinating new incarnation.

Trenzalore, The Doctor's Name, and the Church of the Silence

●● In "The Time of the Doctor," the Doctor defends the farm town of Christmas on the planet Trenzalore with its many innocents. The Time Lords are blasting the question "Doctor Who" through time and space, and if the Doctor replies with his name, they will burst through and restart the Time War. Up above, the Church of the Papal Mainframe and its leader Tasha Lem tries to shield the planet to keep the Doctor's enemies away in a perpetual ceasefire. However, the church also begins a great war with the Doctor:

> TASHA: Attention. Attention all Chapels and Choirs of the Papal Mainframe. The siege of Trenzalore is now begun. There will now be an unscheduled faith change. From this moment on, I dedicate this church to one cause. Silence. The Doctor will not speak his name, and war will not begin. Silence will fall!
> ALL: Silence will fall! Silence will fall.

Strangely enough, this is the arc story's ending and also its beginning.

●● The Doctor mentions the Silents are "Confessional priests. Very popular. Genetically engineered so you

93

forget everything you told them" ("The Time of the Doctor").

➤◄ Prisoner Zero tells the Doctor that "silence will fall" ("The Eleventh Hour"), and these words also appear in "The Pandorica Opens"/"The Big Bang," foreshadowing series six. The date for this event is given as 26 June 2010, when the TARDIS explodes (which indeed makes the universe stop).

➤◄ Madame Kovarian splits off from the Church's true mission and kidnaps Amy then Melody Pond, making the latter into a psychopath who will kill the Doctor and absolutely ensure the question cannot be asked.

➤◄ In the Silents' first appearance, "The Impossible Astronaut," the Silents try to take over earth in 1969 America and also guard a mysterious child in a spacesuit. They already control the planet, and it's implied they are responsible for the Moon landing because they need a special spacesuit for Melody Pond. The Doctor destroys them through a message for humanity added to the video of the moon landing ("Day of the Moon"). Around this time, Amy suspects that she's pregnant, and begins seeing a strange face. The face reappears, and is finally revealed to be Madame Kovarian's, as Amy is no longer with her friends, but trapped on Demon's Run.

➤◄ The Doctor, Amy, and Rory encounter Gangers, Doppelgangers constructed from goo which a human can control from another location ("The Almost People"/"The Rebel Flesh"). At episode end, the Doctor reveals Amy is a Ganger, and has thus left them months before. He promises to find the real her.

➤◄ Having already kidnapped Amy, the Church of the Silence successfully steal baby Melody Pond to raise to destroy the Doctor. In the battle, Colonel Manton lowers the hoods of the headless monks on the authority of the Papal Mainframe – this unseen female head of the order may be Tasha Lem ("A Good Man Goes to War").

- River nearly kills the Doctor, but is convinced to save him with her remaining regenerations ("Let's Kill Hitler").
- In "The Wedding of River Song," the Doctor consults Dorium Maldovar's head in a box to discover the Silence's motives. Dorium tells him "that on the fields of Trenzalore, at the fall of the Eleventh," a question would be asked, a question that must never be answered. It was a creed of the Silence that "Silence will fall when the Question is asked," or as Maldovar translates it, "Silence *must* fall" ("The Wedding of River Song").
- River refuses to kill the Doctor and all of time collapses – in other words, silence falls. In the mashed-up reality, Amy executes Madame Kovarian. River and the Doctor restore reality. He fakes his own death and the Silence appear to be satisfied.

> DORIUM: So you're going to do this? Let them all think you're dead?
> DOCTOR: It's the only way, then they can all forget me. I got too big, Dorium. Too noisy. Time to step back into the shadows.
> DORIUM: And Doctor Song, in prison all her days?
> DOCTOR: Her days, yes. Her nights? Well, that's between her and me, eh?
> DORIUM: So many secrets, Doctor. I'll help you keep them, of course.
> DOCTOR: Well, you're not exactly going anywhere, are you?
> DORIUM: But you're a fool nonetheless. It's all still waiting for you. The fields of Trenzalore, the fall of the Eleventh, and the question.
> DOCTOR: Goodbye, Dorium.
> DORIUM: The first question. The question that must never be answered, hidden in plain sight. The question you've been running from all your life.

Doctor who? Doctor who? Doctor Who. ("The Wedding of River Song")

➤ Clara reads the Doctor's name in *A History of the Time War* but soon forgets it when time is rewritten ("Journey to the Centre of the TARDIS").

➤ A Victorian murderer tells Madame Vastra, "The Doctor has a secret he will take to the grave. It is discovered" and adds the word Trenzalore and coordinates.

> DOCTOR: When you are a time traveller, there is one place you must never go. One place in all of space and time you must never, ever find yourself.
> CLARA: Where?
> DOCTOR: You didn't listen, did you? You lot never do. That's the problem. The Doctor has a secret he will take to the grave. It is discovered. He wasn't talking about my secret. No, no, no, that's not what's been found. He was talking about my grave. Trenzalore is where I'm buried.
> CLARA: How can you have a grave?
> DOCTOR: Because we all do, somewhere out there in the future, waiting for us. The trouble with time travel, you can actually end up visiting. ("The Name of the Doctor")

Nonetheless, he goes, as his friends are in danger. When he arrives, the Great Intelligence tells him his name is the password to his tomb. He refuses to reveal it, but River says it and the tomb is opened. Within the Doctor's timestream, Clara sees the War Doctor, and the Doctor describes his name as a promise and this incarnation as the one who broke the promise.

> DOCTOR: I help where I can. I will not fight.
> OHILA: Because you are the good man, as you call yourself?
> DOCTOR: I call myself the Doctor.
> OHILA: It's the same thing in your mind.

> DOCTOR: I'd like to think so. ("Night of the Doctor")

- "The Day of the Doctor" describes the name as a promise of the sort of man he wants to be: "Never cruel or cowardly. Never giving up and never giving in."
- Ten and Eleven face their past as the War Doctor, forgiving him and acknowledging him as the Doctor at last. Together, they preserve Gallifrey in a pocket universe. Eleven tells Ten he's going to Trenzalore, knowing Ten will forget ("Day of the Doctor").
- In "The Time of the Doctor," the Doctor returns to Trenzalore to discover the Time Lords are calling him through all of time and space with the question "Doctor Who?" If he answers with his real name, they will come through and destroy the universe with another Time War. The Silence fight beside the Doctor to defend Trenzalore for six hundred years.
- Trenzalore in the earlier "The Name of the Doctor" looks different from the one in "The Time of the Doctor." Perhaps history has been changed. Or perhaps River must still have her own gravestone erected over a secret entrance. The Doctor may even return here and die along with his TARDIS...or possibly this future was averted with a new supply of regenerations.

Gallifrey and the Fiftieth Anniversary

Most of this storyline is presented and wrapped up in the same episode

- "The Name of the Doctor" introduces a glimpse of the War Doctor.
- In "The Night of the Doctor," the Eighth Doctor transforms into the War Doctor so he can end the Time War and save the galaxy's innocents.

- Kate Lethbridge-Stewart has the TARDIS with Clara and the Doctor helicoptered to UNIT because a collection of Time Lord art has shattered from within. Elizabeth the First left orders that the Doctor was to be called in case of attack. She also leaves her "credentials," a Time Lord painting of the fall of Arcadia, Gallifrey's second largest city, called "No More" or "Gallifrey Falls."

- In the War, the War Doctor steals the Moment, the worst doomsday device. It projects an image of Bad Wolf at him and warns him he will survive to live with the guilt of all the children he has killed on Gallifrey. She asks, "Do you want to see what that will turn you into? Come on, aren't you curious? I'm opening windows on your future. A tangle in time through the days to come, to the man today will make of you."

- The Eleventh and War Doctors step through to the Tenth, who is dealing with a Zygon invasion in Elizabethan England. The Zygons preserve themselves in Time Lord art until human technology can improve, and they escape in 2013 to invade UNIT's Black Archive where they take the forms on UNIT officers.

- Shut in (but not locked in) the Tower of London by Elizabeth, the three Time Lords talk, and Eleven sends the Vortex Manipulator code to Clara, who takes the device from the Black Archives and uses it. She rescues the Doctors (who have nearly solved the door lock until she points out it's open). Not allowed into the Black Archive, thanks to its tech, Eleven calls Kate's assistant earlier in the episode and has him move the art. Then the Doctors invade through the Gallifrey Falls painting.

- Once there, Ten tells Kate he knows the horrors of destroying innocents and wipes the memory of the humans and their Zygon imitators to make them work out a peace.

- The Moment returns the War Doctor to the doomsday device, lesson learned. However, it also allows Ten and Eleven through to bring him hope and absolution. Once there, however, Clara points out they must be the Doctor and help their people. Eleven realizes there are three of them now.
- Using not just their three incarnations but thirteen of them, they freeze Gallifrey in a single moment in time, held in a parallel pocket universe.
- The three Doctors of the story gather and say their goodbyes. With the words, "Wearing a bit thin. I hope the ears are a bit less conspicuous this time," the War Doctor transforms into Nine.
- The Caretaker, a possible reincarnation or revisiting of the Fourth Doctor, counsels Eleven (It's possible he gave Osgood the scarf). He says the plan worked, and the painting is really titled Gallifrey Falls No More. Eleven goes out to find his people.
- If anyone's aiming for a final count this episode offers…Three TARDISes. Two companions (counting Bad Wolf but not Queen Elizabeth). One companion's descendent (the Brigadier's daughter). One crazed fangirl, times two. Two Fourth Doctor scarves. One fez (that bounces between many timestreams). The second wedding a Doctor has had onscreen. More of the Time War than ever seen. Zygons, Daleks, a Cyberman head. Two giant rooms of doomsday devices. Several time loop paradoxes. 13 Doctors (with some as old footage) 5 Doctors with new footage for the show (and an additional one in "Night of the Doctor"). And the count can go much higher if one includes the lovely scenes from "The Five(ish) Doctors" (with John Barrowman getting a bonus for the driving). If 5, 6, and 7 are indeed hiding in the episode, the count can

go up to a whopping NINE Doctors, from Four through the one who doesn't yet exist, with John Hurt as a bonus in the count. And Doctor Nine is present in spirit as John Hurt regenerates into him.

The Day of the Doctor Easter Eggs

- ▶◀ The original credits, then 76 Totter's Lane and the Coal Hill School begin the episode as they began the series.
- ▶◀ The school sign reads "Headmaster: W. Coburn" and "Chairman of the Governors: I. Chesterton"... Anthony Coburn wrote "The Unearthly Child." Ian Chesterton was a teacher at the school and the Doctor's companion...he might even still work there.
- ▶◀ The clock Clara motorcycles past shows the exact time "An Unearthly Child" was broadcast. And she writes No More on the whiteboard. Hmm....
- ▶◀ They don't dwell on the bit where Clara has met Hurt and Ten before during her splintering into soufflé girl adventure, but that could just be confusing and awkward.
- ▶◀ Smith hanging from the TARDIS mirrors his own first episode *The Eleventh Hour.* Both times dramatic and fun.
- ▶◀ Eleven wears Amy's reading glasses. Ten wears his own "cool" glasses.
- ▶◀ "Reverse the polarity" is the Third Doctor's line.
- ▶◀ Osgood the fangirl is wearing Four's scarf of course. She also uses it as a weapon, as he frequently does.
- ▶◀ Zygons hail from the Fourth Doctor and Sarah adventure "Terror of the Zygons" (in which people dramatically back up when menaced by them, as in this one). This is their first New Who appearance.
- ▶◀ Clara uses Jack Harkness's vortex manipulator. River Song presumably has a different one.

100

- Elizabeth the First and Ten's courtship and wedding (teased in several episodes) are finally shown.
- Even the War Doctor uses a gun to shoot the wall, not the enemy.
- The sealed message from the past, paintings as messages, etc., are seen in "The Pandorica Opens," among others.
- The escape from a dungeon scene nods to many moments, especially Three and Jo scenes.
- The oft-mentioned Time War is shown.
- Gallifrey and the Time Lords' terrible collars. Also their vault of doomsday devices.
- The fez of "The Pandorica Opens," itself a nod to the fez Seven wears, returns (many times over!). Even Ten wears it.
- In "Night of the Doctor," Eight meets the sisterhood of Karn from "The Brain of Morbius," toasts his audio adventures companions, and transforms.
- Earth is doomed to fall to alien invasions, a nod to many many episodes.
- The Moment comes to life with a personality very similar to the TARDIS of "The Doctor's Wife." They're both even wooden boxes.
- Bad Wolf played by Billie Piper returns
- Eleven's signature high-energy theme music
- In UNIT, Clara sees a Cyberman head and a wall of old companion photos, starting with Susan's. River's red sparkly high heels are also there and Amy's "Angels Take Manhattan" pinwheel.
- Hurt: "Timey wimey?" Ten: "I don't know where he gets it from." Ten first said this in "Blink."
- The concept of the Doctor protecting children is emphasized in "The Beast Below" and "The Doctor the Widow and the Wardrobe" among others
- John Hurt regenerates, noting he's "Wearing a bit thin," the words One uses on changing to Two.

- This show uses several of Moffat's signature loops and paradoxes.
- The concept that the Daleks will be terrified of three Doctors. Also, the plan to move Gallifrey so the Daleks all shoot each other is similar to the solution in "Blink."
- Rewriting and preserving timelines
- Obviously, "The Three Doctors," "The Five Doctors" and "The Two Doctors" all dealt with the same sort of paradox and snarky comments towards the other Doctors' dress, mannerisms, etc. It's no wonder Ten isn't shocked to see Eleven after all that.
- This one particularly mirrors *The Three Doctors*, with the old crotchety one complaining about the ridiculous clown and the "cool" charmer. In fact, that was a Brigadier episode, as this is a Brigadier's daughter one.
- Eleven mentions Trenzalore and their fate there
- The need for a Big Red Button
- Daleks daleks daleks
- Ten: "I don't want to go." Eleven: "He always says that." Ten's last words on the show are…still his last words.
- Eleven warns Ten about SPOILERS! for the future…by this point in Ten's life, he's met River and heard her catchphrase in the Library.
- On the Doctor getting kissed: Hurt: "Is there a lot of this in the future?" Eleven: "It does start to happen, yes." A reference to the asexual attitude of the first seven Doctors in contrast with New Who.
- "They're getting younger all the time," Hurt notes (though he thinks Ten and Eleven are companions).
- Eleven has the same phone number as Ten had in "The Stolen Earth." Seems he still has Martha's phone.
- The TARDIS is switched to its original white circles décor. The museum has a similar wall pattern.

- "Is it important?" "In twelve hundred years I've never stepped in anything that wasn't." This actually seems a parody of Eleven's "A Christmas Carol" line that he never met a person who wasn't important. While the latter was sweet, the former just seems silly.
- Kate wants a file from the seventies or eighties. It's murky when UNIT events of the Third Doctor era happened as they were meant to be in the near future (80s), not the present (70s). Hence the date.
- The end credits with the Doctors' faces, is reminiscent of the old style.
- The motorcycle ridden into TARDIS echoes similar stunt riding in "The Bells of Saint John."
- Kate Stewart, daughter of the Brigadier from Three's era (also seen in "The Power of Three") and UNIT. Their Tower of London base is also in "The Power of Three." There's a picture of her father and the Doctor sends a "space-time telegraph" for him.
- The code Eleven scratches into the wall is the time and date *An Unearthly Child* aired. 17-16-23-11-63 – the first *Doctor Who episode* aired at 5:16 p.m. on November 23, 1963.
- Kate is horrified by "Americans with the ability to rewrite history"…this could be a dig at the American *Doctor Who* movie or *Torchwood: Miracle Day* among other things.
- Eleven mentions he lies about his age. This nods to a few inconsistent counts through the series.
- Finally all the Doctors unite to save Gallifrey (which is described by Nine and Ten as "time-locked" so this may actually have already worked. They're seen on screens along with a glimpse of Capaldi, Doctor #12, the first time a Doctor is seen on screen before his regeneration.
- "Hopefully the ears aren't as prominent this time." This nods to the fact that he will soon be Eccleston

(who examines his ears as if he's never seen them in "Rose."

◖◗ The Moment is mentioned in "The End of Time" and several comic books, modified from the De-Mat gun of Four's "The Invasion of Time."

◖◗ And of course, number 4…

UNIT, the Brigadier, and Kate Lethbridge-Stewart

◖◗ The Third and Fourth Doctors are employees of UNIT, as the Time Lords have disabled the TARDIS as punishment for the Doctor's constant interference with other cultures. Companions Liz Shaw, Mike Yates, Jo Grant, and Harry Sullivan work for UNIT as well, though Sarah Jane Smith is a civilian.

◖◗ Kate first appears in the direct-to-video not-quite licensed episode *Downtime* (1995). There is no Doctor, but the Brigadier and companions Sarah Jane Smith and Victoria Waterford appear. The Great Intelligence menaces the Brigadier but also his estranged daughter Kate and grandson Gordon. She followed this with another appearance in *Dæmos Rising* in 2004.

◖◗ UNIT appears in "The Sontaran Strategem" and Martha Jones works for them after leaving the Doctor. They entrust her with the Osterhagen Key and instruct her to use it in "Journey's End," though she does not. Still working for UNIT, she teams up with Jack for a few episodes of *Torchwood* series two.

◖◗ The Brigadier appears in *The Adventures of Sarah Jane*'s *The Enemy of the Bane*, helping her break into the Black Archive.

◖◗ Eleven, rejecting his upcoming death, phones the Brigadier to invite him on an adventure. However, he is informed the man has just died (reflecting the beloved actor's death around this time) and crushed, realizes his own time has come ("Closing Time").

►◄ Rory and Amy meet Kate in "The Power of Three." As Head of Scientific Research, Kate has reorganized UNIT so the scientists are in charge. Eleven Compliments her on continuing her father's work.

►◄ In the Fiftieth Anniversary, Kate is in charge of UNIT. She airlifts the TARDIS to UNIT, following orders from Elizabeth I should the under-gallery ever be under threat. The Zygons, preserved for centuries, break out and infiltrate UNIT, but the Doctor forces her to negotiate a truce with her Zygon counterpart, aided by the fact that both have had their memories wiped. Osgood the Fangirl appears with inhaler, clunky glasses, and Fourth-Doctor scarf, suggesting she's a geek much like viewers. She discovers where the Zygons are hiding and aids Kate in creating a peace.

►◄ Following these events, UNIT, Kate, and Osgood return in "Death in Heaven." Kate kidnaps the Doctor again, this time appointing him President of Earth, against his wishes. Missy kills Osgood (now in a bowtie and insisting "bowties are cool" after her time with the Eleventh Doctor). Kate falls from the plane, but is saved by a Cyberman she is certain is her father, saving the planet one last time.

The Impossible Girl

►◄ The Doctor meets Oswin Oswald, who bakes soufflés and is an entertainment director far in the future ("Asylum of the Daleks"). As it turns out, she died and was transformed into a Dalek. Upon discovering this, she sacrifices herself to save the Doctor, and uses the phrase "Run, you clever boy and remember."

●◄ In "The Snowmen," governess/barmaid Clara Oswin Oswald breaks through the Doctor's grief and demands his help in Victorian London against the Great Intelligence (Richard E Grant). He's charmed, and invites her to travel with him, but she is killed, saving the world in the process. When he sees her grave, the Doctor links her with "soufflé girl" and resolves to track her down.

●◄ The Doctor finds modern Clara when she calls him, thinking the TARDIS's number is a computer help line ("The Bells of Saint John"). She makes a mnemonic of "Run, you clever boy and remember" and creates the nickname "Oswin" from her name, Clara Oswald. However, she appears to be a modern human with no knowledge of her splitting. The Great Intelligence is stealing human minds (making them cry, "I don't know where I am" in a cap to Clara's adventures) and the Doctor defeats him. He discovers her leaf pressed in a book of places she wants to visit, and she describes it as "Page One."

●◄ Clara's parents met "Because this exact leaf had to grow in that exact way in that exact place so that precise wind could tear it from that precise branch and make it fly into this exact face at that exact moment. And if just one of those tiny little things had never happened, I'd never have met you. Which makes this the most important leaf in human history" ("The Rings of Akhaten"). In the episode, she uses it as a bribe on Akhaten, where sentimental value is key. The leaf story likely has yet to conclude – anyone from the Doctor to Clara to River Song may be seen putting it in motion.

●◄ When the Doctor and Clara are trapped in the TARDIS, he interrogates her but discovers she doesn't know why there are copies of her ("Journey to the Centre of the TARDIS")

◘ In "The Silver Nemesis," the kids find pictures of Clara's travels including "The Snowmen," which she has no knowledge of.

◘ "The Name of the Doctor" caps this storyline. The Great Intelligence steps into the Doctor's corpse (of a sort) – a wound in the fabric of time – and attacks the Doctor over and over in all his lives. Clara goes in after him.

> CLARA: If I step in there, what happens?
> RIVER: The time winds will tear you into a million pieces. A million versions of you, living and dying all over time and space, like echoes.
> CLARA: But the echoes could save the Doctor, right?
> RIVER: But they won't be you. The real you will die. They'll just be copies.
> CLARA: But they'll be real enough to save him. It's like my mum said. The soufflé isn't the soufflé, the soufflé is the recipe. It's the only way to save him, isn't it?
> VASTRA: The stars are going out. And Jenny and Strax are dead. There must be something we can do.
> CLARA: Well, how about that? I'm soufflé girl after all.
> DOCTOR: No. Please.
> CLARA: If this works, get out of here as fast as you can. And spare me a thought now and then.
> DOCTOR: No, Clara.
> CLARA: In fact, you know what? Run. Run, you clever boy, and remember me.
> DOCTOR: No. Clara!
> (Clara steps into the time stream. It turns white again.)
> CLARA [OC]: I don't know where I am.
> DOCTOR: Clara!
> (A montage appears of her saving all the different Doctors, advising and protecting them.)
> CLARA [OC]: I just know I'm running. Sometimes it's like I've lived a thousand lives in a thousand places. I'm born, I live, I die. And always, there's the Doctor. Always I'm running to save the Doctor again and again and again. Oi! And he hardly ever

> hears me. But I've always been there. ("The Name of the Doctor")

●◄ The Doctor recklessly enters his own timestream and drags Clara out. He gives her the leaf, saying, "This is you, Clara. Everything you were or will be. Take it. You blew into the world on this leaf. Hold tight. It will take you home."

●◄ The phrase "The Impossible Girl" is used as an identifier in "Deep Breath." Presumably, this name for Clara will still appear, though this arc has been resolved.

●◄ A mysterious woman gives Clara the Doctor's number as a computer helpline ("The Bells of Saint John"). When the Twelfth Doctor flees into Victorian London, he and Clara see an advertisement neither has written, a playful game by an "egomaniac" that convinces them to meet again ("Deep Breath"). In "Death in Heaven," Missy/The Master reveals she did this all. She feels having the Doctor obeying a "control freak" will set him on a path to destroying the galaxy and thus becoming more like his old master. In fact, Clara orders the Twelfth Doctor around with strength and even harshness, using the phrase "Do as you're told."

●◄ Clara finds herself in the Doctor's childhood and comforts him, telling him being scared can lead to great heroism. She also tells him "Do as you're told," and he reacts to this phrase when she says it sometimes in the future.

Clara and the TARDIS Telepathy

> DOCTOR: Trenzalore. I've heard the name, of course. Dorium mentioned it. A few others. Always suspected what it was, never wanted to find out myself. River would know, though. River always knew. Right, come here. Give me your hand. Now,

> the coordinates you saw will still be in your
> memory. I'm linking you into the TARDIS telepathic
> circuit. Won't hurt a bit.
> CLARA: Ow!
> DOCTOR: I lied.("The Name of the Doctor")

- In "Journey to the Center of the TARDIS," the Doctor has Clara bond with the TARDIS. It grows to like her, and sends a "Big Friendly Button" so the Doctor can save it from destruction.
- Clara, seeking her own timeline, bonds mentally with the TARDIS. It takes her to what should have been her childhood, but she is thinking of her problematic date with Danny Pink. Instead she visits him in a children's home and gives him a plastic soldier, persuading him to someday become "Dan the Soldier Man" who protects the helpless ("Listen").
- She then travels to "someone connected with her future." Colonel Orson Pink, an early time traveler from the 22nd century, has traveled to the end of the universe by mistake. He greatly resembles Danny and has the same plastic soldier. One of Orson's great-grandparents told "silly stories," suggesting time travel runs in the family ("Listen"). Clara suspects who he must be, though he doesn't recognize her.
- In "Dark Water," the Doctor instructs her to poor all her love and grief into the TARDIS and track a deceased Danny. This works, and they're taken to an artificial afterlife where human souls are being gathered
- Given the appearance of Colonel Orson Pink, presumably either Danny will return for Christmas or Clara is already pregnant with his child.

Missy's Paradise

- When Doctor Number Twelve is born, he finds himself in Victorian London, battling cyborgs from

109

the sister ship to the Madame de Pompadour from "The Girl in the Fireplace." Their leader insists he's going to paradise, but the Doctor scoffs and says such a place is a myth. The half-faced cyborg dies battling the Doctor and finds himself in a beautiful green garden, presided over by "Missy" ("Deep Breath").

► When Gretchen Carlisle ("Into the Dalek") dies, Missy welcomes her to paradise as well.

► Missy monitors the Doctor and Clara's adventures through the year ("Flatline," "In the Forest of the Night")

► When Danny Pink is killed, the Doctor offers to fly Clara "to Hell" or wherever he is to look for him. Danny has found himself in a series of office buildings overlooking a world of darkness and flame – possibly where Danny fears he belongs, considering the lovely paradise shown in "Deep Breath." He is introduced to a boy he killed by mistake in the Middle East.

► The part where Missy's victims are connected with their bodies and undergo torture as a result appears to be either an act of sadism (possibly intended to convince them to relinquish their emotions and become full Cybermen) or a necessary process to keep them connected with their bodies until they're returned to earth.

► Missy and Danny are sent back to the Nethersphere; Danny has enough power to free one person, but he chooses the child instead of himself.

► Missy will return in series nine.

Repeat Characters

The Great Intelligence

Existing from before the universe, the Great Intelligence constantly seeks physical existence. The Second Doctor calls it "formless, shapeless thing, floating out in space like a cloud of mist, only with a mind and will" (*The Web of Fear*). It also consumes mental energy from its victims as a "mind-parasite" ("The Bells of Saint John"). Yog-Sothoth as it is sometime called exists in living beings as host or in a three-sided pyramid of control spheres (*The Abominable Snowmen*) or ivory (*Downtime*) or once as a giant snowglobe ("The Snowmen").

The Intelligence manifests as a dense fog that consumes all life and a poisonous web spreading through the London Underground in its first appearance (*The Web of Fear*). With a glowing slime that invades earth, the Great Intelligence takes over a Tibetan lama and forces it to build a robot Yeti. In 1935 at the Det-Sen Monastery, the Second Doctor and Edward Travers, a westerner seeking the Yeti, discover it is in fact a machine. They destroy the Yeti and lama together and the world is saved (*The Abominable Snowmen*). In a later video starring the Brigadier and his daughter, it invades every machine and being, cocooning the planet in a massive web (*Downtime*).

In the new series, the Intelligence creates living snowmen in Victorian London, presumably before its Second Doctor adventures ("The Snowmen"). Its avatar Walter Simeon creates the Great Intelligence Institute and sacrifices workers to feed it. In 1892, Clara the governess along with Vastra,

Strax, and Jenny, recruit the Eleventh Doctor to combat it. After Clara's death, her charges begin crying, their tears so sad that the snow turns to rain and melts the snowmen. During this encounter, the Eleventh Doctor shows the Great Intelligence a schematic of the London Underground, inspiring its visit in "The Web of Fear."

It then takes over many human minds through the wireless internet in The Shard during "The Bells of Saint John." At last, it invades the Doctor's entire timestream, sacrificing itself to attempt killing the Doctor (*The Name of the Doctor*). Here it uses the empty-bodied Whisper Men to manifest, though its main form is that of its human avatar Doctor Simeon (Richard E Grant). It is likely that this final strike kills the disembodied monster, though in this series, nothing is final.

The Brigadier

Brigadier Sir Alistair Gordon Lethbridge-Stewart was one of the most prominent recurring characters in *Doctor Who*, appearing in 23 stories during the original series. He appears with many Doctors as, aside from specifically working with Two, Three, and Four, he stars in *The Three Doctors*, *The Five Doctors*, and *Dimensions in Time* (thus meeting One, Five, and Six), then comes out of retirement for *Battlefield* to aid Seven. His actor also stars in Big Finish Audio Adventures.

He first appears in the Second Doctor's adventure *The Web of Fear* (1968). In the Third Doctor's era, he is a regular, giving the Doctor his orders from UNIT and battling the Master by his side. The Fourth Doctor's visits to UNIT are rarer, but the Brigadier is there for his regeneration and beyond. He apparently has romantic feelings for a woman named Doris, mentioned in *Planet of the Spiders*. By *Battlefield*, he has married her. They have a daughter named Kate, seen in several fan films then in the new show. Lethbridge-Stewart retires in 1976 to teach mathematics at Brendon Public School. His successor is Colonel Charles Crichton (*The Five Doctors*).

Though Ten mentions him in the UNIT episode "The Poison Sky," the Brigadier does not appear until 2008 for *The Sarah Jane Adventures*. The actor died in 2011, a moment acknowledged by the Eleventh Doctor's depression in "The Wedding of River Song" as he realizes death comes to everyone. The Twelfth Doctor salutes the Brigadier-reborn-as-Cyberman in the eighth series finale "Death in Heaven," thus achieving some closure. His fictional daughter Kate takes over UNIT and appears in several episodes from 2012 on.

The Master

As the Third Doctor adventures James-Bond style on earth, he is given a perfect nemesis, a Moriarty to his Sherlock Holmes. Roger Delgado, who generally played a sneering, devilish villain, was chosen. (He and Pertwee became close friends.)

In his first appearance, the Master arrives in his own TARDIS (*Terror of the Autons*). He and the Doctor meet and the Doctor steals a TARDIS component, stranding the Master on earth where they have confrontations again and again. He appeared in every episode that year, 1971, and then the writers decided he should take a break as the Master always appeared and always lost, to the point of ineffectualness. It was intended that in an episode called "The Final Game" after the Holmes story "The Final Problem," the Doctor and Master would both die in a grandiose confrontation, but Roger Delgado was actually killed in a car crash before this could occur. The staff chose not to recast the part for three years after, and the Third Doctor regenerates without his nemesis.

The Master returns, horribly scarred and seeking a new set of regenerations in the first Gallifrey episode, *The Deadly Assassin*. The Doctor defeats him but the Master flies away in a TARDIS disguised as a grandfather clock. He returns in *The Keeper of Traken* looking equally foul, still desperate for new bodies. He takes over the body of the Trakenite scientist

Tremas (an anagram of "Master"), and has a new form at last (played by Anthony Ainley). He continues to harass the Fifth Doctor, until in *The Five Doctors*, they become temporary allies, as the Time Lords offer the Master a new regeneration cycle in exchange for his help. He appears again in *Survival*, attempting to defeat the Doctor, failing once more, and ending trapped on the planet of the Cheetah people.

In the 1996 television movie, he's executed by the Daleks and requests that his remains to be brought back to Gallifrey by the Doctor. However, he is able to survive execution in a shapeshifting animal form, and he forces the Doctor and his TARDIS to crash land in San Francisco. He takes over a human paramedic named Bruce (Eric Roberts) then seeks to open the Eye of Harmony on the TARDIS to steal the Doctor's remaining regenerations. Instead, he is sucked into it and apparently killed.

Apparently, the Time Lords resuscitate him to fight in the Time War as one of their most vicious soldiers. In "Utopia," the resurrected Master steals the TARDIS, but is carried unwillingly to October 2006. Arriving in Britain before the Doctor, he (John Simm) takes on the alias of "Mr. Harold Saxon" ("Mister Saxon" is an anagram for "Master No. Six"). He gets himself elected Prime Minister with subliminal messaging and creates the Archangel network, a global low-level telepathic field that allows him to subtly influence the behavior of the world's human population. The Master infiltrates earth though series three of the reboot – he is the one to fund Professor Lazarus's genetic rejuvenation experiments and then interrogate Martha's mother about Martha and the Doctor.

For his great plan, he creates a paradox machine out of the TARDIS to bring the last humans from the end of the universe back in time to destroy their ancestors. He also imprisons the Doctor and tortures his friends for a year. However, the Doctor uses the Archangel Network to focus mankind's belief on himself and use the combined psychic energy of the entire human race to remake his body. He destroys the paradox machine, and the year is banished with it.

Shot, the Master prefers death to regeneration, even as the Doctor pleads with him to live. However, a woman with long, bright red fingernails, one of the Master's disciples, steals a ring from his pyre and uses that, with his human wife Lucy Saxon's DNA to regenerate him. Lucy sabotages the ritual and the Master returns with a failing, undead body (still played by John Simm) in *The End of Time.* He consumes massive amounts of food and can bring down bolts of electricity and jump great distances. He's also madder than ever. Billionaire Joshua Naismith tries using him to repair an alien "Immortality Gate" to make humanity immortal, but the Master reprograms it to turn all of humanity into copies of himself. When the Master learns that his madness and suffering are all from the Time Lords' schemes, he stops Lord Rassilon's attempt to take over earth and apparently follows him into the Time War.

In the eighth series, the mysterious "Missy" (Michelle Gomez) tracks the Twelfth Doctor, creepily identifying him as her "boyfriend." When they meet in person, she kisses him enthusiastically (while the Doctor, stunned, can only ask if it's "over yet"). At the finale, she finally reveals that she is the Master returned ("Dark Water"). She is the one to lead Clara to the Doctor, several times, In her latest scheme, she uses a Matrix Data Slice as a "Nethersphere" to trap the conscious minds of the recently deceased to create more Cybermen than the living humans of earth and overwhelm them. Her second stage plan involves threatening to convert the living humans of earth as well, unless the Doctor takes the cyber army and conquers the galaxy. The "Mistress" appears motivated by obsession with the Doctor – she's determined to prove they're the same and evoke the Doctor's instincts to rule and destroy. The Doctor rejects her threats and her army, defeating her. In a shocking moment, he finally shoots her dead, mostly to stop Clara from doing so. Since it's not entirely clear what her "dissolving weapon" does – it may banish people to the Nethersphere, and there's likely a copy of her there – it's highly likely the Mistress/Master will return once more.

Davros

Sent on a mission to destroy the Daleks just as they're first formed, the Fourth Doctor encounters their original creator. One the greatest scientist of the Kaleds (a suspicious anagram), Davros is confined to a mobile chair that resembles a Dalek itself. He is blind, with his left arm destroyed. He invents the Mark III travel machine, which he thereafter names a Dalek. With the original race mutating, Davros began experiments to determine the Kaleds' final mutated form, developing these "ultimate creatures" to place in the travel machines. By torturing companions Harry and Sarah, Davros forces the Doctor to divulge the future of his Daleks. After, Davros and the Doctor speak scientist to scientist.

> DOCTOR: Davros, for the last time, consider what you're doing. Stop the development of the Daleks.
> DAVROS: Impossible. It is beyond my control. The workshops are already fully automated to produce the Dalek machines.
> DOCTOR: It's not the machines, it's the minds of the creatures inside them. Minds that you created. They are totally evil.
> DAVROS: Evil? No. No, I will not accept that. They are conditioned simply to survive. They can survive only by becoming the dominant species. When all other life forms are suppressed, when the Daleks are the supreme rulers of the universe, then you will have peace. Wars will end. They are the power not of evil, but of good.
> DOCTOR: Davros, if you had created a virus in your laboratory, something contagious and infectious that killed on contact, a virus that would destroy all other forms of life, would you allow its use?
> DAVROS: It is an interesting conjecture.
> DOCTOR: Would you do it?
> DAVROS: The only living thing, a microscopic organism reigning supreme. A fascinating idea.
> DOCTOR: But would you do it?
> DAVROS: Yes. Yes. To hold in my hand a capsule that

contains such power, to know that life and death on such a scale was my choice. To know that the tiny pressure on my thumb, enough to break the glass, would end everything. Yes, I would do it! That power would set me up above the gods. And through the Daleks, I shall have that power! (*Genesis of the Daleks*)

Unfortunately, by programming the Daleks to hate all life forms other than themselves, Davros has engineered his own destruction.

DALEK: All inferior creatures are to be considered the enemy of the Daleks and destroyed.
DAVROS: No, wait! Those men are scientists. They can help you. Let them live. Have pity!
DALEK: Pity? I have no understanding of the word. It is not registered in my vocabulary bank. Exterminate!
DAVROS: For the last time, I am your creator! You must, you will obey me!
DALEK: We obey no one. We are the superior beings.
(*Genesis of the Daleks*)

In fact, Davros is preserved by a backup life support system, and the Daleks brings him back to help in their war against the Movellans. The Doctor defeats Davros and imprisons him in a cryogenic freezer as "a block of ice" (*Destiny of the Daleks*). Nearly a century later, the Daleks free Davros from his prison station so he can help cure a virus the Movellans have introduced among them. Davros secretly attempts to make the Daleks loyal to himself. After the Fifth Doctor reveals his treachery, Davros releases the virus, killing all the Daleks on board before he flees (*Resurrection of the Daleks*).

Davros sets himself up as "the Great Healer" and lures the Sixth Doctor to the planet Necros where he has created an unfailingly loyal race of Imperial Daleks in white and gold. However, the Supreme Dalek's forces arrive and capture him to put him on trial (*Revelation of the Daleks*). In what becomes known as the Shoreditch Incident, Imperial and Renegade Dalek factions battle in this area of London in November 1963. Davros, who has proclaimed himself the Dalek

Emperor, complete with an Imperial Dalek-like shell, seeks the legendary Hand of Omega, but it turns on him and destroys his ship. He flees in an escape pod once again (*Remembrance of the Daleks*). The Doctor bids him goodbye with, "Goodbye Davros. It hasn't been pleasant."

He commands the Daleks in the Last Great Time War, but vanishes when his command ship flies into the jaws of the Nightmare Child (though the Doctor tries to save him). In "Journey's End," it's revealed that Dalek Caan has saved Davros from the Time War. Davros steals 27 planets, including Earth, and stores them in the Medusa Cascade where he uses them to power his reality bomb and destroy all matter in the universe except the Daleks, which he has rebuilt from his own tattered body. The Doctor stops him, and as the ship burns down, the Doctor invites Davros to come with him, but the maddened scientist declines.

The Rani

The Rani is a renegade Time Lord, and recurring villain like the Master. She takes a coldblooded view of science, ignoring those who may be harmed by her actions as long as she can achieve her breakthroughs. The Seventh Doctor says, "She's a brilliant but sterile mind. There's not one spark of decency in her" (*Time and the Rani*). She appears in only *The Mark of the Rani* and *Time and the Rani*, though she also plays the villain in the short charity special *Dimensions in Time* and appears in some audio adventures.

> DOCTOR: And you're so warped, so callous, you think that justifies it? First you turn an innocent young man into your acolyte, force him to betray his friends, and then you do this monstrous thing to him.
> RANI: Oh, stop being sentimental. What's happened? Animal matter has been metamorphosed into vegetable matter. So what?
> DOCTOR: You'll be telling me next he's better off.
> RANI: As a matter of fact, he is. A tree has four times the life expectancy of a human being.

118

> DOCTOR: They should never have exiled you. They should have locked you in a padded cell. Now move, before I forget my abhorrence of violence and use this. (*Mark of the Rani*)

In *The Mark of the Rani*, the Sixth Doctor accidentally lands in Killingworth during the time of the Industrial Revolution. The Rani is stealing the chemical that allows sleep from human brains, in order to give it to her people on the planet Miasimia Goria –where she has removed the need for sleep until the subjects have grown violent. She teams up with the Master, who's only interested in killing his old nemesis. Eventually, the Doctor traps the Rani and the Master in the Rani's TARDIS, with a growing Tyrannosaurus Rex.

In *Time and the Rani*, the Rani traps the TARDIS in a time funnel, injuring the Doctor enough that he must regenerate into the Seventh. The Rani manipulates him by injecting the Doctor with an amnesia drug, and disguising herself as companion Mel (Bonnie Langford). In her exact pink and white outfit with bouncing red hair, the Rani coaxes the Doctor to finish her invention and then tries to steal his mind, along with many great thinkers of the past. Of course, in the end, she's betrayed by her slaves, the monstrous Tetraps, who decide to use her brain for a similar purpose.

In an interview Steven Moffat discussed why he doesn't want to revisit the Rani: "People always ask me "Do you want to bring back the Rani?" No one knows who the Rani is. They all know who the Master is, they know Daleks, they probably know who Davros is, but they don't know who the Rani is, so there's no point in bringing her back. If there's a line it's probably somewhere there" (Caron, "Rani"). Fannish interest suggests this may not be true.

The Valeyard

The Valeyard is, according to the Master, "an amalgamation of the darker side of the Doctor's nature," from somewhere between his "twelfth and final incarnations" (*The Ultimate*

Foe). However, the Doctor may have a second twelfth incarnation. There's also semi-canon work that suggests the Valeyard is an alternate-universe cop[y of the Doctor (*Trial of the Valeyard*). When the Sixth Doctor is on trial for interference with other cultures and genocide, the Valeyard seeks to steal his remaining regenerations (*The Ultimate Foe*). The Valeyard acts as the prosecutor in the Doctor's trial and presents extracts from the Matrix depicting recent past events in the Doctor's life as evidence. However, the Valeyard has tampered with these records. He also plans to destroy the other Time Lords. The Valeyard escapes into the Matrix but the Doctor chases after him and apparently destroys him. The Doctor is acquitted (*The Ultimate Foe*).

> Asked about the mention of the Valeyard in "The Name of the Doctor" and whether it was a hint of things to come: "Well, I couldn't resist saying 'The Valeyard,' because we haven't mentioned him in the new series. [Laughs] So I thought, 'I'll just put that one in.'
>
> He added: "I never quite understood, in 'Trial of a Time Lord,' what he was meant to be. I never understood if he was a real Doctor, or [something else]. But in a story where we are hinting that the Doctor has a hidden chapter to his life, it was irresistible to mention the Valeyard. But you know, he'll only ever get so dark, let's be honest. He's the Doctor. I think a man who worries about going bad is never really going to go bad. Maybe not..." (Anders)

Harriet Jones

The role of Harriet Jones was written specially for Penelope Wilton by Russell T Davies (Craig). She is an "actress who epitomizes all things quintessentially English," appearing in *Calendar Girls* and *Downton Abbey* (Craig).

Harriet Jones is the series' running joke, as everyone, even the Daleks, know who she is. She's first seen surviving the Slitheen attack at Rose's side, as a meek but firm backbench MP who helps to defeat an alien invasion. She has become Prime Minister by the Tenth Doctor's regeneration, and he notes that she is famous for creating Britain's Golden Age.

She bravely defends the earth and reasons with the Sycorax attacking in "The Christmas Invasion." However, after the Doctor saves the day then frightens them off, she engages a worldwide weapon and destroys them.

> DOCTOR: That was murder.
> HARRIET: That was defence. It's adapted from alien technology. A ship that fell to Earth ten years ago.
> DOCTOR: But they were leaving.
> HARRIET: You said yourself, Doctor, they'd go back to the stars and tell others about the Earth. I'm sorry, Doctor, but you're not here all the time. You come and go. It happened today. Mister Llewellyn and the Major, they were murdered. They died right in front of me while you were sleeping. In which case we have to defend ourselves.
> DOCTOR: Britain's Golden Age.
> HARRIET: It comes with a price.
> DOCTOR: I gave them the wrong warning. I should've told them to run as fast as they can, run and hide because the monsters are coming. The human race.
> HARRIET: Those are the people I represent. I did it on their behalf.
> DOCTOR: Then I should have stopped you. ("The Christmas Invasion")

Horrified, he brings her down with the whispered words "Don't you think she looks tired?" It's likely his attack on her allows Harold Saxon to claim the power vacuum he provides.

When the world surrenders to the Daleks and all the companions break down in tears, Harriet Jones activates the subwave network. She is the one who brings the companions together and finally calls the Doctor with it, offering her life to save the planet. Even the Daleks know who she is. She dies threatening them with their downfall at the hands of humanity. Davies wrote her into the episode to give her a satisfying and redemptive conclusion, which certainly is what occurs (Davies & Cook, *Writer's Tale* 382).

Dorium Maldovar (The Blue Guy)

Dorium Maldovar, a black marketer in the 52nd century, sells

River Song a vortex manipulator "fresh off the wrist of a handsome Time Agent." She trades him the disarmer for the micro-explosives she has put in his wine (*The Pandorica Opens*). The Doctor summons him to aid at Demon's Run in *A Good Man Goes to War*. Surrounded by headless monks, he assumes they won't hurt him. He is wrong – they promptly behead him. They meet again in "The Wedding of River Song," as the Doctor goes to him to discover the Silence's motives. Dorium's head in a box tells him that on the fields of Trenzalore, at the fall of the Eleventh, a question will be asked, a question that must never be answered. The Doctor takes his head along on the adventure, and afterwards returns him to the head collection at the Seventh Transept, where presumably he's enjoying the wifi.

The Paternoster Gang

NARRATOR [OC]: In London in the time of Queen Victoria, there were many tales of a remarkable personage known as the Great Detective. I refer, of course, to Madame Vastra, the lizard woman of Paternoster Row and her extraordinary adventures, her beautiful assistant, Jenny Flint, and their mysterious henchman, Strax, whose countenance was too abominable to be photographed. There are also accounts of a fourth member of the Paternoster Gang, a shadowy figure whose assistance was only sought in the direst emergencies. ("The Great Detective" minisode)

Vastra (Neve McIntosh), one of the Silurians sleeping below the earth's crust, is accidentally awoken by an extension to the London Underground. She falls in love with Jenny Flint (Catrin Stewart) and they begin solving crimes together in Victorian London. (She eats the mass-murderers, including Jack the Ripper). The Doctor summons them both to battle in "A Good Man Goes to War." He also summons Strax. As Strax explains in the episode, he serves "a penance to restore the honour of my clone batch. It is the greatest punishment a Sontaran can endure, to help the weak and sick.." The Doctor of course considers this fitting reparations for the events of either the Pandorica or "The Sontaran Stratagem." In "A Good Man Goes To War," Vastra is one of the only characters who dares speak to the Doctor as an equal. Strax, of course, is just hilarious. After the Battle of Demon's Run, the Doctor sends everyone home but Vastra and Jenny invite Strax along:

> VASTRA: The station is being evacuated. We're all being returned to our proper times and places. We wondered if you would like to come with us.
> JENNY: We're from London, 1888.
> STRAX: What of it? Is there something there for me?
> VASTRA: A welcome.
> STRAX: Why?
> VASTRA: We fought together, didn't we, side by side as comrades?
> JENNY: And we couldn't help noticing you do seem to be alone.
> STRAX: I am accustomed to solitude.
> VASTRA: As are we. Jenny here has been ostracised by her family because of, well, let's just say preferences in companionship. I'm the last of my kind as you are the only one of yours. A Sontaran who fought bravely in the best of causes. ("The Battle of Demons Run - Two Days Later" minisode)

They appear as a team in "The Snowmen" as allies of the Doctor, and meet Clara a second time in "The Crimson Horror."

> SIMEON: And her suspiciously intimate companion
> VASTRA: I resent your implication of impropriety. We are married. ("The Snowmen")

They reach out to Clara in "The Name of the Doctor," and the Doctor braves Trenzalore to rescue them. As he tells Clara, "They cared for me during the dark times. Never questioned me, never judged me, they were just kind. I owe them. I have a duty. No point in telling you this is too dangerous"("The Name of the Doctor"). They return for the

Twelfth Doctor's first episode in order to help Clara bridge the transition to the new Doctor.

> CLARA: You said renewed. He doesn't. He doesn't look renewed. He looks older.
> VASTRA: You thought he was young?
> CLARA: He looked young.
> VASTRA: He looked like your dashing young gentleman friend. Your lover, even.
> CLARA: Shut up.
> VASTRA: But he is the Doctor. He has walked this universe for centuries untold, he has seen stars fall to dust. You might as well flirt with a mountain range.
> CLARA: I did not flirt with him.
> VASTRA: He flirted with you.
> CLARA: How?
> VASTRA: He looked young. Who do you think that was for?
> CLARA: Me?

As Vastra adds, "The Doctor regenerated in your presence. The young man disappeared, the veil lifted. He trusted you. Are you judging him?" ("Deep Breath"). With her counsel, Clara learns to see the Doctor beneath. Invited to join the team, she instead chooses to keep traveling with the new Doctor.

Osgood the Fangirl

This character, a scientist at UNIT, first appears in the fiftieth anniversary special. With a Fourth-Doctor scarf, big clunky glasses, and an asthma inhaler, she appears to be the perfect fangirl – a young geek in a labcoat representing millions of devoted fans. She is quite brave and discerning when the Zygons attack.

She returns in the Twelfth Doctor's series eight finale, "Death in Heaven." This time in true fangirl form she wears an Eleventh Doctor bowtie and spouts the line "bowties are cool," much as fans do at every conference. Unfortunately, the Doctor obliquely invites her to travel as his companion. In episodes from "Voyage of the Damned" to "The Girl in the Fireplace" to "The Snowmen," the Doctor's inviting a young woman to travel with him can signal her immediate death. Missy kills her with a chilling line that she kills for the same reason people pop a balloon – because it's pretty, like Osgood. While her boss Kate survives, Osgood appears to have permanently perished.

Kate Lethbridge-Stewart

Kate first appears in special direct-to-video not-quite licensed episode *Downtime* from 1995. There is no Doctor, but the Brigadier and Sarah Jane Smith appear (played by their original actors), along with companion Victoria Waterford. The Great Intelligence menaces the Brigadier but also his estranged daughter Kate and grandson Gordon. She follows this with another appearance in *Dæmos Rising* in 2004. Intriguingly, she makes it from the spin-off into the mainstream when she appears at Rory and Amy's house in "The Power of Three." As Head of Scientific Research, Kate reorganizes UNIT so the scientists are in charge.

For the Fiftieth Anniversary special, she is the one who orders the airlifting of the TARDIS to London, as she claims she is following orders from Elizabeth I should the under-gallery ever be under threat. She negotiates a truce with her Zygon counterpart, aided by the fact that both have had their memories wiped so are determined to be fair to the other side. She is willing to destroy all of London to prevent aliens from taking the Black Archive, and displays a strong ruthlessness, as well as trust in the Doctor.

In "Death in Heaven," she knocks the Doctor out upon meeting him, then has him carried to an official plane and appoints him President of Earth. Missy tries to kill everyone on the plane, but when the dead of earth return as Cybermen, Kate's father appears to be one of them, saving Kate by retaining his human emotions.

Organizations

UNIT

> ELEVENTH DOCTOR: Unified Intelligence Task Force.
> CLARA: Sorry?
> DOCTOR: This lot. UNIT. They investigate alien stuff. Anything alien.
> CLARA: What, like you?
> DOCTOR: I work for them.
> CLARA: You have a job?
> DOCTOR: Why shouldn't I have a job? I'd be brilliant at having a job.
> CLARA: You don't have a job.
> DOCTOR: I do. This is my job. I'm doing it now.
> CLARA You never have a job.
> DOCTOR: I do. I do.("The Day of the Doctor")

In fact UNIT has never revoked the Doctor's credentials. He works for them as the Third and Fourth Doctor – as he is stranded on earth, the British government decides to make use of him as a scientific advisor who in practice performs many James-Bond like acts of heroism. Much later, Martha Jones becomes a soldier and medical officer under their command.

UNIT, originally the United Nations Intelligence Taskforce, is introduced in the Second Doctor's era, along with the beloved Brigadier, who starts the task force to protect the planet from alien incursions (*The Invasion*). It is a military group under the command of the United Nations. The Doctor, exiled to earth and suddenly regenerated into his third body, agrees to become their scientific advisor. Liz

THE CATCHUP GUIDE TO DOCTOR WHO

Shaw and Jo Grant, Unit officers, become the Doctor's assistants, and Harry Sullivan joins the team for backup. Around this time, the Master attempts numerous schemes on earth, and UNIT eventually imprisons him with the Doctor's help (*The Dæmons*). With his exile finally ended, the Doctor only occasionally returns to help out UNIT (*The Three Doctors*) through his third and fourth incarnations (*Planet of the Spiders, Robot, Pyramids of Mars*). The Seventh Doctor reunites with UNIT to battle Morgaine and her knights. By now, there is a female brigadier in charge, Winifred Bambera, though Lethbridge-Stewart is called out of retirement to assist (*Battlefield*).

In the new series UNIT returns to investigate the Slitheen in Downing Street. They also have a secret prison where they keep Toshiko Sato until Jack Harkness recruits her and bargains for her release ("Fragments"). They have a command center in the Tower of London under the command of Major Richard Blake in 2006 ("The Christmas Invasion"). They own an aircraft carrier airship, the *Valiant*, actually designed by the Master ("The Sound of Drums"/"Last of the Time Lords"). In "The Sound of Drums," U.S. President-Elect Winters states that UNIT protocols for alien first contact were established in 1968; this was the year UNIT entered the series.

They return in "The Sontaran Stratagem," now with Martha in their ranks. Martha, on loan from UNIT, also collaborates with *Torchwood* series two and with the Doctor in "The Stolen Earth"/"Journey's End." With reverse-engineered future tech, she uses UNIT's Project Indigo, a teleportation device and considers activating UNIT's Osterhagen Project, in which three out of five UNIT facilities can end humanity's suffering by destroying the planet with nuclear weaponry under Earth's crust. The Doctor requests she dismantle it.

During Easter 2009, the Doctor works with UNIT when a bus travels through a wormhole. Scientific adviser Professor Malcolm Taylor is quite eager to help, and after a firefight,

128

the Doctor recommends to the taskforce leader Captain Erisa Magambo that there might be potential UNIT recruits from the bus ("Planet of the Dead"). UNIT also investigates the return of the 456 alongside Torchwood in *Children of Earth*.

Sarah Jane Smith maintains friendly contact with UNIT, seeking out the Brigadier and the Black Archives in *Enemy of the Bane*. Kate Lethbridge-Stewart, the Brigadier's daughter, appears in "The Power of Three" and reveals that she, and thus the scientific arm, is now in charge. With the base in the Tower of London, she leads UNIT during the Fiftieth Anniversary special and the Twelfth Doctor's "Death in Heaven."

Time Agency

The Time Agency exists from roughly the 49th century through the 52nd century ("Kiss Kiss, Bang Bang"). They employ human Time Agents with vortex manipulators for quick and dirty time travel.

This first appears in *The Talons of Weng-Chiang* as the villain uses his Time Cabinet to murder and manipulate in Victorian London but fears the Time Agents will come to arrest him for breaking time travel laws:

> WENG: Bah. Those dumb-witted oxen. Chang, I have given you mental powers undreamt of in this century. You are thousands of years ahead of your time. What can you fear from these primitives?
> CHANG: True, Lord, I read their minds with ease, but tonight there was a stranger, a man whose thoughts were hidden. A man different from all others.
> WENG: Describe him.
> CHANG: He is a doctor. Tall with wide pale eyes and hair that curls like the ram. He asks many questions.
> WENG: A time agent would not ask questions. A time agent would know.

Jack Harkness, rogue Time Agent, is introduced in "The Empty Child"/"The Doctor Dances." He describes himself as losing faith and leaving them after the Agency wipes two years of his memory for undisclosed reasons (which in fact are never revealed in four years of *Torchwood*). His vortex manipulator features in many episodes, and he soon takes over Torchwood Three. In series two of *Torchwood*, another agent, calling himself John Hart, appears on earth and tells him the agency is falling apart ("Kiss Kiss, Bang Bang").

Torchwood

The Torchwood Institute is founded by Queen Victoria in 1879 to defend the earth from alien threats. She names it after the Torchwood estate where she meets the Tenth Doctor, though the name, an anagram for Doctor Who, was used by Davies to hide what his new show was going to be. However Victoria's creation also seeks to acquire and modify alien tech by any means necessary and modify it into deadly weapons. They also investigate the Doctor and have no trust for him ("Tooth and Claw").

In 1899 Cardiff, the local branch is run by Alice Guppy and Emily Holroyd, who recruit a time traveling Captain Jack as a freelance agent. He is disturbed by their brutality as they execute a blowfish alien but he serves them for a century, as he cannot die but must continue to wait for the Doctor, who only arrives in the twenty-first century ("Fragments").

Jack visits New York in the 1920s, as seen in a *Miracle Day* flashback. In 1965, Jack, as a Torchwood agent, gives twelve children from an orphanage to the aliens known as the 456 as a gift (*Children of Earth*). In 1999, Jack inherits Torchwood Three when one of its members, Alex Hopkins, kills the rest of the team and himself after encountering an alien artifact that reveals his future ("Fragments").

With an unofficial slogan of "If it's alien, it's ours," they design the galactic cannon seen in "The Christmas Invasion" (2006). They are a running plot thread through the new series two, as Yvonne Hartman plots to reestablish the British Empire. Torchwood Tower at Canary Wharf opens a rift to gather free energy, but an army of Cybermen come through and destroy and convert the workers of Torchwood, destroying Torchwood One ("Army of Ghosts"/ "Doomsday").

Torchwood Two is reportedly based in Glasgow, run by one man whom Jack Harkness regards as "very strange." Torchwood Four has been "lost" and will likely reappear ("Everything Changes"). In the books, there's a Torchwood India as well. The organization appears to be semi-secret, as many ordinary people and institutions know of it.

Following his adventures with the Doctor, Captain Jack Harkness decides to run Torchwood Three in a way that will make the Doctor proud, defending the earth altruistically and bravely. He works with the Doctor and Sarah Jane in "The Stolen Earth"/"Journey's End," though Sarah Jane comments that she doesn't care for his team's violent methods. He teams up with UNIT in series two as Martha Jones visits for a few episodes and he donates his vortex manipulator to their Black Archive ("The Day of the Doctor"). Their base is destroyed in *Children of Earth*, and they basically go underground. Finally, the CIA drags them to America to investigate the events of Miracle Day. Torchwood reportedly still exists in the 42nd century as the Torchwood Archive ("The Satan Pit").

Species

Daleks

Despite the producer's rule against "bug-eyed monsters," Terry Nation wrote the second episode of *Doctor Who*, which he titled *The Daleks*. This only was made because of the determination of Verity Lambert (combined with the amount of money that had already gone into the Daleks). The episode had eight million viewers, the largest ever for a BBC program. Children were playing Daleks on the street, and the classic villains were permanently established. Terry Nation received literally thousands of letters and continued writing the Daleks' adventures. As he explains, "They represent government, officialdom, that unhearing, unthinking, blanked-out face of authority that will destroy you because it wants to destroy you" (Haining 21).

> DALEK 1: Over five hundred years ago there were two races on this planet. We, the Daleks, and the Thals. After the neutronic war, our Dalek forefathers retired into the city, protected my our machines.
> DOCTOR: And the Thals?
> DALEK 1: Most of them perished in the war, but we know that there are survivors. They must be disgustingly mutated, but the fact that they have survived tells us they must have a drug that preserves the life force. (*The Daleks*)

Early on, the eyestalks were vulnerable, and Daleks glided, unable to climb stairs. These weaknesses, however, were eliminated from later models. They could float and fly as early as the Seventh Doctor's encounter (*Revelation of the*

THE CATCHUP GUIDE TO DOCTOR WHO

Daleks). The Cult of Skaro developed armor with temporal shift technology ("Doomsday"). The term "rel" as a Dalek unit of time first appeared in the Peter Cushing movies then the Expanded Universe, before it was used in "Doomsday." The creatures inside their "machines" are almost always Kaled mutants, which the Seventh Doctor once describes as "little green blobs in bonded polycarbide armour" (*Remembrance of the Daleks*). Occasionally they kidnap other species, mutate them, and put them in the casings (as shown first in "Asylum of the Daleks").

Parts of the shell include a gun mount containing an energy weapon ("gunstick" or "death ray") and a telescopic manipulator arm (resembling a plunger). This last can interface with technology, crush a man's skull, and extract information from a person's mind.

They are arrogant and fanatical, determined to wipe non-Dalek creations from the earth, even their flawed, non-Dalek creator. Those Daleks that are a threat are promptly eliminated. When the First Doctor meets them on Skaro, he learns that they are stranded survivors of a neutronic war who have become dependent on the radiation, unlike the more human Thals still hiding in the forests ("The Daleks"). They can only move thanks to static electricity from the metal floors. Fighting beside the Thals, the Doctor and his friends wipe them out.

However, the Daleks soon return. Led by the Dalek Emperor and a Supreme Commander, they conquer and occupy the Earth in the 22nd century. They attempt to replace Earth's core with a propulsion system, turning the planet into a spaceship, but they are thwarted once more (*The Dalek Invasion of Earth*). After leaving their own planet, the Daleks add dishes to their casing to receive power (*The Dalek Invasion of Earth*), then an ability to move without them.

The Daleks develop time travel and formed an interstellar (and later intergalactic) Dalek Empire (*The Daleks' Master Plan*). The Dalek Supreme sends an execution squad through time to kill the First Doctor, chasing him from far-off planets to New York City in 1966 (*The Chase*). In *The Evil of the Daleks*, they force the Second Doctor to implant the Human Factor into three Daleks. The Doctor does so, but encourages his new creations, Alpha, Beta, and Omega, to defend their own lives. The worried Emperor orders the Daleks through an archway that will reimplant the Dalek Factor. However, the Doctor reverses the technology so the human factor is implanted instead. Civil war thus breaks out on Skaro. However, the humanized Daleks are defeated and the Daleks build a new command structure with grey drones and gold Supreme Daleks (*Day of the Daleks*).

Encounters between the Doctor and the Daleks continue as the Daleks war with other races. Eventually, the Doctor is sent to destroy the Daleks at the moment of their creation, but cannot bring himself to do it (*Genesis of the Daleks*). The Daleks attempt to duplicate the Fifth Doctor to assassinate the Time Lord High Council (*Resurrection of the Daleks*). After, Davros begins to turn cryogenically frozen people into Imperial Daleks but the Renegade Daleks battle him and win (*Revelation of the Daleks*). The Imperial and Renegade Daleks battle on Earth in 1963 in what is later called the Shoreditch Incident. There, Davros accidentally destroys his own soldiers, while the Seventh Doctor convinces the last Renegade Dalek, the black Supreme Dalek, into self-destructing (*Remembrance of the Daleks*).

The Great Time War falls, with Time Lords and Daleks tearing apart all of reality with their hideous war machines. At last, the Doctor activates the Moment, destroying both sides and trapping them, time-locked together forever. Despite this, the Ninth Doctor stumbles across a single dying survivor in "Dalek" and realizes the depth of his irrational hatred.

In "Doomsday," four particular Daleks appear:

> ROSE: Doctor, they've got names. I mean, Daleks don't have names, do they? One of them said they
> DALEK: I am Dalek Thay.
> BLACK DALEK: Dalek Sek.
> DALEK 3: Dalek Jast.

DALEK 2: Dalek Caan.
DOCTOR: So that's it! At last. The Cult of Skaro. I thought you were just a legend.
ROSE: Who are they?
DOCTOR: A secret order above and beyond the Emperor himself. Their job was to imagine, think as the enemy thinks. Even dared to have names. All to find new ways of killing.

Dalek Caan returns in "Journey's End," now insane after viewing time itself. He flies into the Time War, rescues their creator Davros and escapes. Now a prophet, Dalek Caan secretly begins to undermine the Dalek regime as he understands the truth of their evil. Meanwhile, Davros begins creating a new Dalek race from his own body. They try to destroy the universe in the series four finale, but the Doctor and Donna stop them.

In "Journey's End," all Dalek saucers are destroyed, but a single one survives. It flies back in time to World War II, where one of the progenitors (a device containing pure Dalek DNA) is located. However, with new DNA from Davros, the Daleks do not appear "pure" or "true" Daleks. In "Victory of the Daleks," they invent a robot supervisor and construct an elaborate plan so the Doctor, on arrival, bellows, "I am the Doctor, and you are the Daleks." Thus the Progenitor is activated by this eyewitness testimony. It creates a new race of Daleks, the Paradigm Daleks, who gain new technology – in "Asylum of the Daleks," and after, the Dalek utilize Nanogenes to turn humans into Dalek Puppets.

These last were once humans or similar races, but are killed by the Daleks and transformed. They often forget their deaths and conversion, convinced they're still human. When activated, they find a miniature eyestalk protrudes from their foreheads and a gunstick or light beam bursts from the hand. Oswin Oswald's crew are converted this way in "Asylum of the Daleks," as is Tasha Lem ("The Time of the Doctor"). The Robomen, humans mind-controlled by Daleks, likely anticipate this process (*The Dalek Invasion of Earth*).

Cybermen

The Cybermen first appear in the serial *The Tenth Planet* in 1966, set in 1986, in which their origin story is given as follows. Millennia ago, during prehistoric times, Earth had a twin planet known as Mondas. Mondas was knocked out of solar orbit and drifted into deep space. The Mondasians, already far in advance of Earth's technology and fearful for their race's survival, replaced most of their bodies with cybernetic parts. Having eventually removed all emotion from their brains, to maintain their sanity, the natives installed a drive propulsion system so they could pilot the planet itself through space. As the original race was limited in numbers and were continually being depleted, the Mondasians – now Cybermen – became a race of conquerors who reproduced by taking other organic beings and forcibly changing them into Cybermen.

These Cybermen fight against the First Doctor when the Cybermen attempt to drain the Earth's energy to make way for Mondas' return to the solar system. However, Mondas absorbs too much energy from Earth, destroying it and those Cybermen on Earth. The adventure takes its physical toll on the Doctor, forcing him to regenerate for the first time.

They return in "The Moonbase," this time with much more robotic costumes as though "money had been spent on them," as producer Innes Lloyd said at the time (Haining 58). The story was nearly a perfect copy of *The Tenth Planet*, to try to keep audience enthusiasm from the first serial. They are most terrifying because of their lost humanity – Peter Davison said in an interview, "Once it happens, once you become a Cyberman, you're not coming back. You can't just put your organs and the bits of your brain they took out back in. It's a terrifying idea, losing your identity as you become a killer" (Kistler 68).

The Cybermen also have cybernetic weapons known as "cybermats." In their first appearance in *The Tomb of the Cybermen*, they resemble giant metallic silverfish with segmented bodies and crystalline eyes. The Second Doctor calls them a "form of metallic life." Other cybermats appear in *The Wheel in Space*, able to tune in on human brainwaves. The Second Doctor jams them with an audio frequency. *Revenge of the Cybermen* has larger, snake-like cybermats that can inject poison into their victims.

After losing the Cyber-Wars, the Cybermen attempt to destroy the humans' gold-rich asteroid Voga and take back their power. The Fourth Doctor meets a small group of the latest redesign in *Revenge of the Cybermen* (1975). In *Earthshock* (1982), the Fifth Doctor encounters Cybermen trying to destroy 2526 Earth and the ongoing peace talks. Adric sacrifices himself, stopping them in another encounter, and the cyber ship crashes, taking the place of the meteor that killed the dinosaurs.

The 1980s Cybermen wore converted flight suits painted silver, in contrast to the earlier random tubing and cloth and rubber diving suits. The iconic handle bars on their heads remained throughout. The time-traveling Doctor meets the Cybermen out of sequence, but often the later episodes have more elaborate Cybermen irrespective of when they are supposed to live. Various fan guides attempt to address the contradiction, positing the Cybermen may have time travel capabilities.

Attack of the Cybermen (1985) precedes *Revenge*, as the Cybermen face defeat from humanity's glittergun and the discovery of gold-rich Voga. In *Silver Nemesis* (1988), a cyberfleet try to convert Earth into a new Mondas. They seek the legendary Nemesis statue, a Time Lord artifact of immense power, made of the "living metal" validium. The Seventh Doctor and Ace stop them.

The Cybermen return in 2006 with a new origin story on the alternate earth known informally as Pete's World. The new Cybermen are burnished steel with an art deco design. In the "Rise of the Cybermen"/"The Age of Steel" two-part story, the owner of Cybus Industries, the dying transhumanist mad scientist John Lumic (Roger Lloyd Pack) has converted the world's population by placing their human brains into robotic shells. The Tenth Doctor and his friends free London with aid from the human resistance group, the Preachers. In the 2006 finale "Army of Ghosts"/"Doomsday," the Cybermen invade earth and battle the Daleks, before the Doctor banishes them all into the void between worlds. "Cyberwoman" on *Torchwood* sees Ianto Jones (Gareth David-Lloyd) trying to save his girlfriend, partially converted during these events. The Christmas Special "The Next Doctor" has Cybermen invade 1851 London after the walls of reality are damaged.

Cybermen appear as ensemble enemies in *The Five Doctors* (1983), *Dimensions in Time* (1993), "The Pandorica Opens," "A Good Man Goes to War," and "The Time of the Doctor." Abandoned cyber heads appear in many more episodes, especially including Eleven's companion Handles.

In "Closing Time," an ancient crashed cyber ship with cybermats is reawakened in 2011 Colchester; thus, cybermats are reintroduced to the series. Neil Gaiman's "Nightmare in Silver" has Cybermen reappearing in the distant future, much stronger and faster. The Eleventh Doctor undergoes a partial cyberconversion, and mentally duels with a Cyber-Planner for control of his body. In the 2014 finale, "Dark Water"/"Death in Heaven," the Cybermen ally with the Master, who offers them the bodies of earth's dead in 2014. Several resist the programming and turn heroic.

Ice Warriors

The Second Doctor, Jaime, and Victoria meet the Ice Warriors in the 1967 serial of that name. These creatures from Mars try to conquer the Earth but the Doctor defeats them. They try to escape to Earth's Ice Age. In *The Monster of Peladon* (1974), other more benevolent Ice Warriors appear. When confronted by alien sentient water in the 2009 episode "The Waters of Mars" the Tenth Doctor theorizes that the Ice Warriors froze it in an underground glacier to prevent its escape, calling them "a fine and noble race who built an empire out of snow."

The 2013 episode "Cold War" features the return of the Ice Warriors as on a sunken Soviet submarine Eleven faces Grand Marshal Skaldak, a legendary warrior trapped in the ice for 5000 years. He believes humanity has declared war on him and tears apart crew members to study the weaknesses of human anatomy. He prepares to detonate the sub's nuclear missiles and destroy the planet, but finally relents. All are rescued by an Ice Warrior spaceship that pulls the submarine to the surface. Moffat comments:

> Mark Gatiss had been pitching the Ice Warriors for a while. I wasn't tremendously persuaded. I thought they were maybe the default condition for what people thought of as rubbish Doctor Who monsters: things that moved very slowly and spoke in a way that meant you couldn't hear a word they said. I thought maybe that was the definitive rubbish one. But then Mark came up with a couple of very clever ideas. It's an absolute cracker of an episode. (Roth "Why Moffat Was Against Bringing Back Ice Warriors")

Silurians

The Silurians are scientifically advanced sentient humanoids descended from the dinosaurs, first appearing in the 1970 serial *Doctor Who and the Silurians*, created by Malcolm Hulke. Since the time of the dinosaurs, the Silurians have been in self-induced hibernation. In the episode, they are awakened by a nearby nuclear power research center. The Doctor negotiates a compromise with the colony's leader, but that leader is assassinated by his son, who desires are more aggressive policy. The Silurians plot to release a deadly virus and radiation, but the Third Doctor thwarts them. In an ambiguously moral moment, UNIT destroys their base. The 1972 serial *The Sea Devils* also by Hulke introduces their amphibious cousins, awakened by the Master. The Sea Devils declare war, forcing the Doctor to destroy their base.

The land-based Silurians and the Sea Devils return, united, in *Warriors of the Deep* (1984), once again trying to reclaim Earth from the humans. The Fifth Doctor tries to prevent any bloodshed but Turlough kills the last survivor, leaving the Doctor despondent. Heavily redesigned Silurians are reintroduced to the series in 2010, in the two-parter "The Hungry Earth"/"Cold Blood." Awakened by an underground drilling operation in 2020, the worried Silurians take hostages. These Silurians lack the third eye of their 1970–1984 counterparts, and wear masks. They are called *Homo reptilian* in "The Hungry Earth" (2010). The Eleventh Doctor negotiates a peace and convinces the Silurians to go back into hibernation. He leaves behind two humans to act as ambassadors when the Silurians re-awaken in a thousand years.

They return as the Doctor's enemies in "The Pandorica Opens" and "The Time of the Doctor" alongside many other species. "Dinosaurs on a Spaceship" features a Silurian Ark searching for a new planet with a cargo of dinosaurs, though the Silurian colony on board has perished.

Madame Vastra (Neve McIntosh) is a recurring character, introduced in "A Good Man Goes to War," then solving crimes in Victorian London thereafter with her human companion and wife Jenny Flint with the Sontaran Strax as butler. The "Paternoster Gang," as the three are known, appear in "The Snowmen," "The Crimson Horror," "The Name of the Doctor," and "Deep Breath."

Autons

The Autons are an artificial life form originally created by Robert Holmes. They kicked off the third Doctor's first adventure (and the first color episode) *Spearhead from Space* (1970), as a warning about modern technology. The image of store mannequins coming to life and shooting people down in the street became an iconic *Who* image and one of the early moments of everyday objects turned terrifying.

These life-sized plastic dummies, animated by the alien Nestene Consciousness, are named for their dummy company, Auto Plastics. They can duplicate living people, whom they generally keep alive to maintain the copy. *Terror of the Autons* features more aspects of normal life turned monstrous, like a police officer really an Auton under his mask. The Master, in his first appearance, steals a Nestene device from a museum and takes over a plastics factory where he organizes the production of deadly Auton dolls, chairs and daffodils.

Autons feature in episode one of the revival, "Rose," as a nod to the first revival as the show turned to color. They attempt to destroy the human race and consume all the pollutants on the planet, with their own planets vanished. Rose kills the main consciousness with a vial of the Doctor's "anti-plastic" solution. The dummies that attack in "The Christmas Invasion" seem like a similar nod as the emblems of Christmas shopping come to terrifying life. The Autons appear in "Love & Monsters" in a pseudo flashback to Rose's adventures. Meanwhile, Rory and many of Amy's childhood fantasies are duplicated as Autons to create a trap for the Doctor in "The Pandorica Opens."

Zygons

Zygons are solidly built humanoids with large, cone-shaped heads. Their heads, arms and torsos are covered in suckers, and they have deeply inset faces. They can take "body-prints" and copy another person's form, though they must keep the person preserved and renew the copying process every two hours. In their original appearance in *Terror of the Zygons* (1975), the episode used an electronic effect generator for the intermediate stage of transformation, appearing as a man-shaped swirl of color.

These sucker-covered creatures return in "The Day of the Doctor." Their planet has been destroyed in the Time War and they're seeking another – they arrive in Elizabethan England and infiltrate London, but decide to preserve themselves in Time Lord art, emerging from stasis when the world is more evolved and comfortable to live in. This they do in 2013, but Doctors Ten and Eleven foil them, along with the War Doctor and Clara. Ten and Eleven mindwipe the Zygons and their human doubles, forcing them to all negotiate a perfect compromise and peace agreement, since they don't know which side they're actually on.

Moffat told interviewers: "Every year since I took over [Doctor Who] I've been trying to get the Zygons in. And then I thought 'Well, it's the 50th...' "The Zygons are beautifully designed monsters, they are so wonderful... We barely changed the design at all because it was so good." As he adds, "And in a way it was fun to bring back Doctor Who's biggest monster success ever, the Daleks, and then go to maybe the smallest monster success [the Zygons] – they were only in it once but everyone remembers them – great monsters, great outfits... and they have these nice whispery voices..." (Caron, "Zygons").

Sontarans

The Sontarans are humanoids with a stocky build, greenish brown skin, three fingers per hand, and a distinctive dome-shaped head. As they're squat and dense thanks to their heavy gravity world of Sontar in the "southern spiral arm of the galaxy," one soldier in "The Sontaran Stratagem" describes one as "a talking baked potato."

In "The Sontaran Stratagem," the Doctor nevertheless calls them "the finest soldiers in the galaxy." Every aspect of their society is bent toward warfare, as in *The Sontaran Experiment*, the Fourth Doctor comments that "Sontarans never do anything without a military reason." In the episode "The Poison Sky," it is revealed that the Sontaran Empire have been at war with the Rutan Host for more than 50,000 years, and which in present day (2008), they are losing.

In *The Time Warrior*, Linx states that "at the Sontaran Military Academy we have hatchings of a million cadets at each muster parade." The Doctor notes in *The Invasion of Time* that Sontarans can clone themselves at a million embryos every four minutes. From the moment they reach adulthood, the Sontarans are sent to battle. Becoming a healer for the sick is one of their most demeaning jobs and dying in battle is

THE CATCHUP GUIDE TO DOCTOR WHO

a triumph. All the Sontarans have monosyllabic names, many beginning with an initial 'st' sound such as Styre, Staal, Skorr, and of course Strax.

The Sontarans' weak spot is the "probic vent" at the back of their neck, through which they draw nutrition. They must always advance in battle, as retreat would leave their necks exposed – in fact any sort of sharp blow will knock them out.

Rutans
These ancient enemies of the Sontarans are quite different from their nemeses. One Rutan appears in *Horror of Fang Rock*, though they are mentioned in some of the Sontaran episodes. They resemble large green jellyfish that create and absorb electrical energy and can change their forms to resemble anyone they wish.

Slitheen
The Slitheen are a criminal family of Raxacoricofallapatorians. Their rivals and cousins are the Blathereen family (*The Gift*). They try to take over the British government in "Aliens of London" and destroy the world from Cardiff in "Boom Town," both times with nuclear explosions. They aid in imprisoning the Doctor in the Pandorica and fighting him at Tranzalore. One drinks at the bar near Captain Jack in *The End of Time*.

The alien species use a compression field to shrink into human skinsuits harvested from their victims. In *The Sarah Jane Adventures,* they perfect smaller skinsuits. Goofy and conniving, they are repeat villains on this show, as they attempt to drain the sun (*Revenge of the Slitheen*), reprogram Mr. Smith to kidnap Luke from his mother (*The Lost Boy*) and steal K9 (*From Raxacoricofallapatorius with Love*).

> SARAH JANE: The outcast Slitheen Family are scavengers, thieves of others technology. Known to infiltrate low-tech planets by hiding in the skins of the dominant native species. Slitheen in Downing Street.
> LUKE: What?

144

SARAH JANE: Something a friend said once. Gas
exchange from skin compression often results in
LUKE: Farting. Farting's funny. (*Revenge of the Slitheen*)

More Slitheen attempt to crush the Earth into a giant
diamond but are stopped by the Blathereen (*The Gift*). In
another incident, they try to kill Sarah Jane with a bomb but
Clyde and K9 save the day (*The Nightmare Man*).

Raxacoricofallapatorians are large and green, or
sometimes orange-brown. They run quite fast and their sense
of smell is officially the best in the galaxy (*Revenge of the
Slitheen*). Vinegar will melt them, as Rose and Nine discover
early on, because they are made of calcium.

Ood

The Ood, a humanoid species with tentacles on their faces,
are a telepathic race, terribly vulnerable with an external brain
held in their hand. Slavers captured them and replaced this
brain with a "translation sphere" to communicate with non-
telepaths. On other occasions, strong telepaths have taken
over the bodies of the Ood, turning their eyes red. As the
Doctor notes, "The Ood are harmless. They're completely
benign. Except, the last time I met them, there was this force,
like a stronger mind, powerful enough to take them over"
("Planet of the Ood"). The Ood insist they require no names
or titles as they are connected to a hive mind and function as
one unit. Their telepathy resembles a beautiful chorus of
song.

They first appear in *The Impossible Planet* as a slave race,
described as wishing to serve others. The group called
"Friends of the Ood" who oppose Ood slavery are
mentioned in the episode. The Tenth Doctor fails to save
their lives, and guiltily recalls this on their next encounter.
This is the series four episode "Planet of the Ood," in which
Donna and the Doctor discover the key to their slavery and
save them, by releasing the immense Ood hive mind from
Ood Operations. The Ood insist, "The circle must be
broken," and the Doctor finally understands this and releases

the dampeners around the brain. "Stifled for two hundred years, but not anymore. The circle is broken. The Ood can sing," he notes triumphantly. After being freed, all Ood across the universe are returned to the Ood Sphere. Ood Sigma prophecizes to the pair, mentioning the "Doctor-Donna" and warning that the Doctor will die soon. He also transforms their slavemaster into an Ood himself.

> DOCTOR: Funny thing, the subconscious. Takes all sorts of shapes. Came out in the red eye as revenge, came out in the rabid Ood as anger, and then there was patience. All that intelligence and mercy, focused on Ood Sigma. How's the hair loss, Mister Halpen?
> (More hair comes away in Halpen's hand.)
> HALPEN: What have you done?
> DOCTOR: Oh, they've been preparing you for a very long time. And now you're standing next to the Ood Brain, Mister Halpen, can you hear it? Listen.
> HALPEN: What have you? I'm not.
> (Halpen's face goes blank. He drops his gun, reaches for his head and peels the skin off. Then tentacles come out of his mouth.)
> DONNA: They, they turned him into an Ood?
> DOCTOR: Yep.
> DONNA: He's an Ood.
> DOCTOR: I noticed.
> (Halpen sneezes and a small hind brain flops into his hands.)
> SIGMA: He has become Oodkind, and we will take care of him.
> DONNA: It's weird, being with you. I can't tell what's right and what's wrong any more.
> DOCTOR: It's better that way. People who know for certain tend to be like Mister Halpen.

Ood Sigma appears again in the 2009 specials to presage the Doctor's death. *The End of Time* welcomes the Doctor into the circle of the Ood to see his upcoming future.

A single Ood appears in "The Doctor's Wife," once again taken over by a strong telepath and then sacrificed. Einstein is transformed into an Ood in the minisode "Death is the Only Answer," while in the minisode "Pond Life," the Doctor accidentally leaves an Ood at the Ponds' house, who insists on becoming their butler.

Clockwork Robots

In the 51st century, the repair droids of the SS Madame de Pompadour try to repair their wrecked ship by cannibalizing the crew in grotesque fashion. They open time windows to the time of the actual Madame de Pompadour, intending to use her brain as their computer, but the Tenth Doctor prevents them ("The Girl in the Fireplace"). They dress in 18th century French clothing to blend in, with clockwork controls so they can function even without ship power.

Their sister ship, the Marie Antoinette, crashes in Earth's distant past. In the Victorian era, they try to fix the ship with both organic and mechanic material so they can reach the "promised land." They use spontaneous combustion to cover their murders. Though the newly-regenerated Twelfth Doctor cannot remember the droids, he defeats them ("Deep Breath").

Judoon

The Judoon are galactic police serving the Shadow Proclamation. They first appear in the episode "Smith and Jones," brutally interrogating earth humans by dragging them to the moon and conducting an investigation until the people there have nearly suffocated. They are unintelligent and the Doctor calls them little more than "interplanetary thugs."

With rhinoceros heads and bulky bodies under bulky armor, they have an enormous lung capacity and yellow blood. Judoon who appear on the moon is an in-joke from the scriptwriter – with David Tennant's Scottish accent, one of the harder sounds to pronounce with an English accent is the 'oon' sound, including the line "a Judoon platoon upon the Moon."

In *Prisoner of the Judoon* on *The Sarah Jane Adventures*, the Judoon Captain Tybo crashes on earth and his prisoner escapes. Tybo sets out to hunt him down, while enforcing sound and speed limits for other drivers on the road.

> RANI: Come on, we've only got ten minutes until Judoon
> enter Earth orbit.
> TYBO: Judoon will secure building. Androvax trapped.
> RANI: Yeah? And what about Sarah Jane?
> TYBO: Humans irrelevant.
> LUKE: How can you say that? Sarah Jane's my mother.
> TYBO: Halt!
> RANI: What?
> TYBO: Do not infringe directive.
> (Tybo points to the 'have you paid and displayed' notice.)
> CLYDE: What? You've got to be kidding.
> TYBO: You pay. You display. (*Prisoner of the Judoon*)

Judoon imprison the Doctor in the Pandorica in "The Pandorica Opens," but fight by the Doctor's side in "A Good Man Goes to War."

Weeping Angels

The Weeping Angels are a predatory race introduced in "Blink" (2007). The Doctor says that the Weeping Angels "are as old as the universe (or very nearly), but no one really knows where they come from." He also calls them "the deadliest, most powerful, most malevolent life-form ever produced." As the Doctor repeats his message, "Don't Blink," Sally Sparrow defends herself against the creature, who become inert stone angel statues that are "quantum-locked," then move when no one is observing them. When they're close enough, claws and sharp fangs appear as the angel takes on a frighteningly savage appearance and springs. They can take power from electric lights or even the TARDIS. If they don't find energy, they are permanently trapped as statues. They have a very strong grip and move incredibly quickly.

They kill their victims somewhat bloodlessly, by taking them so far into the past that they are dead of old age in the present. The angels then feed off the energy created by the time paradox. They are "the only psychopaths in the universe to kill you nicely," as the Doctor adds. The episode was so acclaimed that they had many more appearances. Moffat attributes their appeal to childhood games such as Grandmother's Footsteps or Simon Says and the notion that every statue might secretly be a disguised Weeping Angel (*Doctor Who Confidential*).

River and Eleven face them in "The Time of Angels"/ "Flesh and Stone," in which it's revealed that an image of them can come to life and take over a person from inside their eyes. "That which holds the image of an angel becomes itself an angel." The Doctor also opens a dialogue with them, though they sadistically mock and torment him with those he cannot save. He finally reverses the gravity and throws them all into the Crack in Time to close it.

In "The Angels Take Manhattan," cherubim, or giggling baby angels appear, but these are just as deadly. The Statue of Liberty is revealed as an angel as well. Finally, the angels take Rory and Amy into the time-locked past, from which they can never return. They cameo in "The God Complex," a story about fear. Several angels also attack Eleven and Clara in creepy fashion, emerging from the snow in "The Time of the Doctor."

Weevils

"Weevils" are the name given to monsters from the rift that are a staple on *Torchwood*. Jack Harkness notes that this is a nickname – he and his team don't know what the race call themselves as the snarling creatures are "not too good at communicating" ("Everything Changes"). He shows one to Gwen to convince her alien life is real. The Torchwood team captures them in the sewers and generally imprisons them. The weevils are very strong and mildly telepathic, also very sensitive to paradoxes in time. They are especially vulnerable to high sounds, electricity, and Torchwood's anti-Weevil spray. They appear to worship death, as ancient woodcuts illustrate a Weevil dressed as the Grim Reaper and they cower before Owen Harper after his resurrection ("Dead Man

Walking"). They help imprison the Doctor in the Pandorica.

Teselecta

In the episode "Let's Kill Hitler" Justice Department Vehicle Number 6018 appears. This vehicle, disguised as a human being, is actually a ship of miniaturized people on a mission to execute the worst criminals in history. Eleven, Amy, and Rory accidentally save Hitler from this fate. The Doctor states that the Teselecta use "Basic miniaturization sustained by compression field" (much like the Slitheen's) to fit 423 people into a human-sized body. They can miniaturize others and bring them inside the ship, though the "Antibodies" (floating killer robots) will kill anyone onboard without "privileges." Upon discovering infamous murderer River Song, they attempt to bring her to justice instead. The Eleventh Doctor also uses one of their ship-bodies to escape his own death ("The Wedding of River Song").

Items

Human Tools

Contact Lenses

The Torchwood team have special contact lenses, which allow their headquarters to see through the eyes of their agents, complete with a lip-reading program. Martha Jones wears it in "Reset" and several agents use it in "Children of Earth" (while Gwen, Rhys and Ianto all reveal they've all used the Contact Lenses for "personal use"). In *Miracle Day* (2011), Gwen says they are the only piece of Torchwood technology they managed to keep. Called Eye-5 lenses, they're used in several episodes and finally hacked, though they're normally untraceable by earth technology. The Torchwood team also have earpieces for communication.

Cryo-chamber

Torchwood stores its corpses here indefinitely – Suzie Costello is placed in storage until she comes back to life later, and Jack, presumed dead, is stored in "End of Days" and "Exit Wounds."

Gangers

Gangers (Doppelgängers) are human clones created from an artificially created organic substance called the Flesh. Humans can operate their clones through telepathic remote control, allowing the clones to do more dangerous activities, such as mining. They become popular in the22nd century. ("The Rebel Flesh"/"The Almost People"). However, due to a freak accident, when the acid-mining facility at St John's Monastery is hit by a solar storm, the active Gangers gain independent thought and rebel against their creators. At episode end, after the Doctor and his own ganger negotiate a peace, it is revealed that Amy Pond has been replaced by a Ganger – it has been going on the adventures, while she, mentally linked to it, actually lies captured by the Church of the Silence and Madame Kovarian.

Gravity Globe

Gravity globes float in the air and create gravity. If opened, anti-gravity material spills out and cancels the gravity of whatever it touches. The Eleventh Doctor throws gravity globes to reach the Byzantium, which was 30 feet above him, in "The Time of Angels."

Nanogenes

Microscopic robots are used medically in "The Empty Child" and "The Doctor Dances," to return soldiers to health on the battlefield. They are Chula technology, and have a disastrous effect on mankind, producing zombielike creatures modeled after the "Empty Child." In "Asylum of the Daleks," and after, the Dalek utilize Nanogenes to turn humans into Dalek Puppets.

Nitro-9

Ace, the Seventh Doctor's companion, has invented this explosive device, which she carries in her backpack in aerosol spraycans, and uses in battle.

Osterhagen Key

The Osterhagen (an anagram of "Earth's Gone") key was unvented by UNIT. 25 nuclear warheads placed are beneath the Earth's crust, with activation stations in Alaska,

Argentina, China, Germany and Liberia. Martha explains in "The Stolen Earth", that the Osterhagen Key is to be used "if the suffering of the human race was so great, so without hope, then it became the final option." The Doctor is horrified and demands Martha get rid of the system.

Progenation Machine

In "The Doctor's Daughter" the device copies the Doctor's DNA and produces a direct descendant, his daughter Jenny. She arrives fully adult and trained with language, battle, and other skills.

Resurrection Gauntlet

The Torchwood team uses a mysterious gauntlet from the Rift to bring back the dead for just a few minutes. It is linked with a knife, both made from an unidentifiable metal. It has an empathic link with its wearer, like "a rope from [the] heart to the glove" and that transfers the life force of the wearer to keep the dead alive. Suzie Costello, researching it, becomes obsessed with death and turns murderous ("Everything Changes") and continues this pattern when the glove briefly brings her back ("They Keep Killing Suzie"). Only Suzie and Gwen have enough empathy to use it. It's destroyed, but Ianto points out that "gloves come in pairs," implying that there may be another. In "Dead Man Walking," the second glove appears and revives Owen Harper for far longer than the other glove can.

Retcon/Amnesia pill

The Torchwood team regularly uses these to make people forget supernatural occurrences. They were developed by Torchwood One under Yvonne Hartman. In a poignant moment, Gwen Cooper feeds Rhys retcon after confessing her affair with Owen.

Phones and Calling the Doctor

Past companions have no way of contacting the Doctor again – Sarah Jane expresses her fury to the Tenth Doctor at being ditched in the wrong city and waiting decades for his return. Jo echoes her:

> JO: I only left you because I got married. Did you think I was stupid?
> DOCTOR: Why do you say that?
> JO: I was a bit dumb. Still am, I suppose.
> DOCTOR: Now what in the world would make you think that, ever, ever, ever?
> JO: We'd been travelling down the Amazon for months, and we reached a village in Cristalino, and it was the only place in thousands of miles that had a telephone, so I called you. I just wanted to say hello. And they told me that you'd left, left UNIT, never came back. So I waited and waited, because you said you'd see me again. You did, I asked you and you said yes. You promised. So I thought, one day, I'd hear that sound, Deep in the jungle, I'd hear that funny wheezing noise, and a big blue box right in the middle of the rainforest. You see, he wouldn't just leave. Not forever. Not me. I've waited my whole silly life. ("Death of the Doctor," Part 2)

The Doctor reveals he's silently watched over his former companions, but this stresses the one-way nature of communication. On leaving, Mel shows the difficulty:

> MEL: I'll send you a postcard!
> SEVENTH DOCTOR: But I don't have an address.
> MEL: Oh, I'll put it in a bottle and throw it into space! It'll reach you... in time. (*Dragonfire*)

All this changes in Rose's time. The Doctor adjusts Rose's cellphone in "The End of the World," allowing it to dial through time and space. He notes it can "call anyone, in any time, so long as you know the area code." Rose gives the phone to Mickey Smith at the end of "The Age of Steel" (when leaving him in another dimension!), but soon gets another. The Tenth Doctor upgrades Martha's phone in "42" and she leaves it with the Doctor in "Last of the Time Lords," insisting he pick up if she calls (the phone number, 07700 900461, was reportedly called over 2000 times during "Journey's End").

The Doctor also upgrades Donna Noble's phone, and Barclay's phone in "Planet of the Dead." Amy and Rory's phones, upgraded offscreen, are used throughout the series. Sarah Jane and the children have cellphones on their own series, but, as a repeating theme of their adventures, their phones are always confiscated or destroyed. In "The Man that Never Was," Luke explains to Sky that he's had seven phones in the last four years.

Brigadier Lethbridge-Stewart gives the Doctor a space-time telegraph (of all things) that can contact the Doctor anywhere. The Doctor receives its signal at the end of *Revenge of the Cybermen*, and returns to battle to Zygons. The telegraph is later stored in the Black Archives in "The Day of the Doctor," and the Doctor uses it to reach Kate Stewart, the Brigadier's daughter.

In "The Empty Child"/"The Doctor Dances," Jack Harkness and the Empty Child use an Om-Com, which allows communication through anything with a speaker grille, even the TARDIS's external police box phone. The TARDIS phone receives calls in several other episodes, especially "The Bells of Saint John."

Preacher Gun

These can destroy Daleks and Cybermen, and are used by the alternate universe Preachers in finales to series two and four.

Sonic Blaster/Square Gun

Jack Harkness's beloved blaster carves a large square hole in walls. Rose calls it a "squareness gun" because of its blast pattern (The Doctor Dances). River uses a sonic blaster, which may even be the same one on her first appearance ("Silence in the Library"/"Forest of the Dead").

Time Lord Tools

3D Glasses

The Tenth Doctor uses red-blue 3D lenses to examine the "Void Stuff" and apparent ghosts in "Army of Ghosts," as they reveal the void's background radiation. Jack Harkness keeps a pair on his desk ("Small Worlds").

Biodamper

This screens the wearer from detection. The Doctor gives Donna a ring as biodamper in "The Runaway Bride," proclaiming, "With this ring, I thee biodamp." A boy also wears one in *The Sarah Jane Adventures* episode "The Empty Planet" – in fact, he's an exiled half-alien prince who must remove the ring his father gave him and replace his father as ruler of a planet.

Cubes

The message cube appears in "The War Games" with disturbing messages from other Time Lords. It returns decades later in "The Doctor's Wife" as the Doctor receives ancient cries for help.

The D-Mat Gun

The Dematerialization Gun, from *The Deadly Assassin,* can remove the target from space-time. In the comics, the Doctor resolves to recreate this gun, or rather, something bigger, to end the Time War.

The Moment

This Gallifreyan super weapon is locked away by the Time Lords because of its apocalyptic power. The Doctor takes the Moment from its vault with the intent to use it to end the Time War ("The End of Time"). This moment of time is explored in "The Day of the Doctor," as the device takes the form of Rose Tyler/Bad Wolf and examines his motivations. He finally discovers a way to end the Time War without destroying Gallifrey.

Mirror Detector

Upon meeting Van Gogh and a mystery monster, Eleven pulls out a species matcher, which can identify a species by image. He adds that he had thought it a useless gift from a dull two-headed godmother with bad breath. It shows the Doctor's first two incarnations but misinterprets the beast, a Krafayis. The Doctor appears to abandon it in the church after the monster smashes it, but likely collects it before leaving.

Paradox machine

The Master creates a Paradox machine in "The Sound of Drums," using the Doctor's TARDIS to prevent the universe from collapsing under the logical contradiction of a grandfather paradox when the Toclafane kill their ancestors, modern day humans. Destroyed, it reverses time back to the point of its creation, as occurs when Jack Harkness shoots it with an assault rifle.

Pocket watch/Chameleon Arch

The Chameleon Arch "rewrites biology," making someone like a Time Lord appear to be a different species, complete with new memories. The Tenth Doctor uses it in "Human Nature," transforming into the human school teacher, John Smith. His old personality is sealed in a fob watch. In "Utopia," Martha discovers that the Master has used the same process to survive to the end of time.

Psychic Paper

The Ninth Doctor (and subsequent Doctors) uses a blank card in a travel holder to convince people of whatever he wants them to see – mostly aliases and credentials. He uses it as his invitation to "The End of the World" when first introducing it in the episode of that name. It can apparently unlock electronic pass readers ("Army of Ghosts") and record transit fares ("Planet of the Dead"). Torchwood Institute personnel train in overcoming its suggestion, and William Shakespeare sees through it in "The Shakespeare Code," suggesting his high intelligence.

The Doctor receives messages on it from Jack and River, along with aliens in distress. Occasionally its results are goofy and imprecise. In "The Empty Child," Jack Harkness accidentally uses it to show Rose he's single and available. In "A Christmas Carol," the Doctor tries using it to prove he's a responsible adult, but this is "a lie too big" for the paper.

Rassilon's Goodies

The Five Doctors shows the Black Scrolls, filled with forbidden knowledge from the Dark Time of Gallifrey. In *The Five Doctors*, the Harp of Rassilon is accompanied by a painting that shows Rassilon himself playing it. Playing the tune on the sheet music there unlocks a secret door leading to the Time Scoop controls.

The De-mat gun which features in *The Deadly Assassin* requires the Great Key of Rassilon as an ingredient. Its location is known only to the Chancellor of the High Council of Time Lords. Finally, the Lord President of Gallifrey in "The End of Time" disintegrates dissenters with a frightening gauntlet. He is Rassilon somehow returned to life for the Time War.

Sonic Screwdriver

In the Second Doctor's *Fury from the Deep*, he pulled out a sonic screwdriver to open a hatch. "Neat, isn't it," he comments. Thereafter he uses the device with an increasing set of functions, from sensing radiation to remote-detonating landmines.

The sonic screwdriver is used by the Second and Third

Doctor, and then vanishes after 1982, as it was too powerful and thus hampering the storytelling. In the Fifth Doctor serial *The Visitation*, a villain destroys it, with the Doctor protesting, "I feel as if you've just killed an old friend." In "Time Crash," the Tenth Doctor jokes about the Fifth Doctor's lack of screwdriver, noting that he "went hands-free" and could "save the universe using a kettle and some string."

It reappears in the 1996 movie and "Night of the Doctor" with a telescopic mechanism, then fully returns for the new series. It appears to use soundwaves to exert physical forces on objects remotely. On the new show, it is indeed a cure-all, able to repair machines, cut or fuse many substances, intercept and send signals, operate the TARDIS by remote, or even heal injuries.

It's the Doctor's favorite tool in the new series, though characters tend to mock it. In "The Doctor Dances," Jack Harkness, armed with a sonic blaster, asks, "Who looks at a screwdriver and thinks, 'Ooh, this could be a little more sonic'?" and adds that "in a pinch, you could put up some shelves!" In "Day of the Moon," River Song says he can't help in battle because, as she puts it, "You have a screwdriver! Go build a cabinet." The screwdriver is useless against wood or deadlock seals (introduced in "Bad Wolf"). In "Forest of the Dead," the Doctor mentions a few hair-dryers can interfere with it, though he adds that he is "working on that."

In "Let's Kill Hitler" the Eleventh Doctor has a sonic cane. The Sixth Doctor in *Attack of the Cybermen* uses a "sonic lance" as a remote detonator to explode an unstable material. In *Robot*, a different sonic lance is added to the sonic screwdriver. The Time Lady Romana makes her own sonic screwdriver, smaller and sleeker than the Doctor's, in *The Horns of Nimon*.

Jack Harkness has a sonic blaster ("The Empty Child") and Scaroth has a sonic knife used to steal the Mona Lisa in *City of Death*. Sarah Jane has a "sonic lipstick." Miss Foster in "Partners in Crime" has a sonic pen that can unlock doors.

The Doctor throws it in the trash. Gwen Cooper appears to have a similar one in *Children of Earth,* which she uses to deactivate CCTV cameras. She calls it a "Gizmo."

Time Scoop

The Time Scoop was invented in Gallifrey's "dark times" to capture aliens and make them fight to the death for the Time Lords' pleasure (*The Five Doctors*). The Time Lord Borusa uses this to capture Doctors One, Two, Three, and Five, while trapping Four in an endless time loop. He also collects a number of companions and monsters such as a Dalek, Cybermen, and Yeti (*The Five Doctors*). Another Time Scoop appears in *Invasion of the Dinosaurs,* used to transport dinosaurs to the 1970s to attack London. This device has also appeared in novels and audio adventures.

Timey-Wimey Detector

The Tenth Doctor constructs a temporal disturbance detector in "Blink" and calls it this jokingly. As he adds, it "goes ding when there's stuff". He also says it can boil eggs at thirty paces, whether the user wants it to or not, and that he has therefore learned to avoid hens, because it is not pleasant to be around them when they explode. When he and Martha Jones are sent back to 1969 without the TARDIS by the Weeping Angels, he uses this definition, apparently to joke about translating time travel theory into layman's terms. The device incorporates a lunchbox, some tape reels, a telephone handset, a postcard, and the Doctor's sonic screwdriver. Another version of this machine returns in "The Day of the Doctor," which the Doctor now also claims can "download comics from the future." The War Doctor mocks his childish labeling methods.

Time Travel

TARDIS

> DOCTOR: It's called a chameleon circuit. The TARDIS is meant to disguise itself wherever it lands, like if this was Ancient Rome, it'd be a statue on a plinth or something. But I landed in the 1960s, it disguised itself as a police box, and the circuit got stuck.
> MICKEY: So it copied a real thing? There actually was police boxes?
> DOCTOR: Yeah, on street corners. Phone for help before they had radios and mobiles. If they arrested someone, they could shove them inside till help came, like a little prison cell.
> JACK: Why don't you just fix the circuit?
> DOCTOR: I like it, don't you? ("Boom Town")

When the show began in 1963, the TARDIS was introduced as a commonplace police box, found all over Britain. As such, it suggested that the most ordinary of sights could reveal untold wonders and indescribable powers, as two human teachers wander into a junkyard, enter the TARDIS, and are swept off into a world of adventure. One critic notes, "The dramatic contrivance of such an advanced and seemingly magical form of technology also being imperfect adds to the charm of the show, as does the bizarre imagery of a British police box acting as a spaceship" (Kistler 52).

However, nowadays Police Boxes are no longer used – in fact the police lost the trademark for the boxes to the BBC when a judge ruled that the police had abandoned the design while *Doctor Who* continued using it for decades. The first two Doctors' boxes have a St. John's Ambulance badge on one door, vanished until the ship's rebuild in "The Eleventh Hour." The Bells of Saint John (an episode and monastery) seem something of an homage.

The TARDIS, "Time And Relative Dimensions In Space," can travel through time, space, and (rarely) alternate universes and dimensions. It is bigger on the inside than the outside. It can travel anywhere in the universe that isn't Time-Locked, such as the Time War. In "The Impossible Planet" it's established that TARDIS's are grown, rather than built, with the last seeds for them destroyed in the Time War.

The Third Doctor calls it "dimensionally trans-cendental" to indicate that it's larger inside. The Fourth Doctor explains its being out of sync with the universe as a "state of temporal grace." Eleven uses the same words to explain why Melody Pond cannot shoot someone while inside – when she does shoot, he admits that his line is a "clever lie" ("Let's Kill Hitler"). In the fifth Doctor's era, weapons are also fired inside.

Several stories indicate TARDISes were invented to observe the universe in perfect camouflage, though the Doctor breaks the rules by interfering. The Ninth Doctor adds that when he leaves the ship, he becomes part of the local timeline.

The Doctor's TARDIS has a chameleon circuit that allows it to blend in with its surroundings, but this is broken, stuck on Police Box setting (presumably the Doctor likes it this way). Despite the broken circuit, the TARDIS can still turn invisible as shown in *The Invasion* and "The Impossible Astronaut." The Doctor repairs this feature at one point, but only for the length of an episode.

> ADRIC: So the chameleon circuit's stuck?
> DOCTOR: Exactly.
> ADRIC: In Totter's Yard.
> DOCTOR: In a totter's yard. Anyway, it was ages ago. It doesn't matter. She was in on Gallifrey for repair when I borrowed her.
> ADRIC: I thought she was yours?
> (The Doctor gets underneath the console.)
> DOCTOR: Well, on a sort of finders-keepers basis, yes. I should have waited till they'd done the chameleon conversion, but there were other pressing reasons at the time. (*Logopolis*)

An out-of-date "Type 40 Travel Capsule," it was in a

repair shop when he stole it, accounting for some of its quirks. In the earlier episodes, the Doctor appears to have no ability at all to control where and when he travels. The reboot episodes show him in perfect control…except when the TARDIS inexplicably diverts them because of an emergency or distress call. When the Time Lords give the Third Doctor permission to resume his travels (after grounding him on earth for several seasons) they also give him a new dematerialization circuit that (most likely) allows him to choose his destinations at last.

Inside, the hexagonal console surrounds a Time Rotor, which rises and falls in the old series, then becomes a tall cylinder with rising and falling tubular devices for the movie. Spinning disks replace this later. During the Ninth and Tenth Doctors' times, the hexagon is replaced with a six-part circle, though the Eleventh returns to a hexagon. The Tenth Doctor says in "Journey's End" that six people are meant to fly it (no wonder he has such trouble in early episodes!). Stations include vector trackers, dimensional stabilizers, force field generators, scanner controls, and mustard and ketchup nozzles.

The TARDIS is much bigger inside, with a maze of bedrooms and corridors, and a special wardrobe for the Doctor with many classic costumes. By the 1970s, the Fourth Doctor and his companions find a swimming pool, jungle room with man-eating plant, and an extensive drawing room with a pair of boots in it called the Boot Cupboard. There's also a library, cloister garden, and rooms for all its guests. There's a "Zero Room" shielded from the rest of the universe, where the Fifth Doctor recovers from his regeneration in *Castrovalva*. 2013 shows a technology tree that can grow anything needed.

> DOCTOR: No! No, no, stop! Please, don't. Don't touch it. Please. She won't let you touch it. I can feel a TARDIS tantrum coming on.
> GREGOR: What the hell is this place?
> DOCTOR: Architectural Reconfiguration System. It

163

reconstructs particles according to your needs.
GREGOR: A machine that makes machines?
DOCTOR: Yes, basically. ("Journey to the Centre of the
TARDIS")

The TARDIS exterior, often referred to as a "shell," is most likely just a kind of projection from the null-space in the time/space vortex where the TARDIS interior lives.

Components include the Atom Accelerator (an orb with pins radiating from it) that steers the ship ("The Curse of the Black Spot") and the dematerialization circuit, which allows travel. The relative dimensional stabilizer, or RDS, bridges the "dimensional barrier" between the interior and exterior of the ship. The First Doctor steals the "dimensional control" from the Monk's TARDIS in *The Time Meddler,* making the interior too small to enter.

The Cloister Bell is a church bell of a sort located in the Cloister Room inside the TARDIS, which sounds to warn the inhabitants of catastrophe. The Fourth Doctor tells his young companion Adric that he can summon the Doctor by sounding the Cloister Bell. However, it sounds on its own in the episode, indicating the Doctor will soon die and possibly destroy the universe in the process (*Logopolis*). When the Fifth Doctor arrives, the bell rings as the TARDIS is travelling back in time to Event One (*Castrovalva*) and when the TARDIS is trapped in a Dalek time corridor (*Resurrection of the Daleks*).

The Tenth Doctor regenerates erratically, and the Cloister Bell sounds as the TARDIS crashes on earth ("Children in Need Special") and again when the Master turns it into a paradox machine ("The Sound of Drums"). It sounds when the Tenth Doctor and Fifth Doctors meet ("Time Crash"), when the universe is ending ("Turn Left"), and when the Doctor's death approaches ("The Waters of Mars").

The Eleventh Doctor's regeneration also crashes the TARDIS and sounds the bell ("The Eleventh Hour"). It sounds again when the Siren teleports the TARDIS aboard her home ship ("The Curse of the Black Spot"), when House takes it over ("The Doctor's Wife") and when a pair of scavengers steal it ("Journey to the Centre of the TARDIS"). The TARDIS sounds the alarm when the Doctor's "greatest fear" attacks ("The God Complex") and when he's trapped in a pocket universe ("Hide"). It chimes twice when the Great Intelligence enters the Doctor's tomb and then his timestream ("The Name of the Doctor"). Other moments include the Twelfth Doctor fainting ("Deep Breath," "Listen") and the TARDIS entering siege mode ("Flatline").

More normally, it produces the TARDIS's classic sound, which the Doctor calls "the sound of the universe" ("Love and Monsters"). River says this sound is produced because the Doctor leaves the break on, but she may be joking or incorrect as other TARDISes make the same sound. Brian Hodgson of the BBC Radiophonic Workshop created the sound by running his mother's old front door key up and down the bass strings of an old piano, then altering the sounds in production.

The Eye of Harmony, an artificially created black hole, is used as a power source in the movie and in "Journey to the Centre of the TARDIS." The Doctor also charges the TARDIS at the Cardiff Rift for as long as it's open.

A perception filter convinces everyone nearby to ignore the otherwise blatant police box. The field extends to objects associated with the TARDIS, such as its keys and other items like fob watches. After the TARDIS recharges at the Cardiff rift, it leaves a square of cement with a perception filter, so the Torchwood team makes it into their hidden entrance. In "Last of the Time Lords" Martha Jones uses her TARDIS key's filter to protect her, while villains use one in "The Vampires of Venice" "The Lodger," "Night Terrors," and "The Eleventh Hour."

The Doctor often claims the TARDIS is "alive," and it actually heals itself after it crashes after the Eleventh Doctor's regeneration. The TARDIS communicates telepathically with the Doctor and Companions, especially in its feature as a translator on alien planets. In the third serial, *The Edge of*

Destruction, Ian asks whether the TARDIS can think, and the Doctor vaguely suggests it can. He's calling it "old girl" by his third incarnation.

> DOCTOR: Hmm? Oh, other times, other places. Well, come on, old girl. There's quite few millennia left in you yet.
> ROMANA: Thank you, Doctor.
> DOCTOR: Not you, the TARDIS. (*The Horns of Nimon*)

By the Twelfth Doctor's Christmas special "The Snowmen," he's added an interface so the TARDIS can speak to him. He also tries to get Clara and the TARDIS to be friends:

> CLARA: You're not getting me to talk to your ship. That's properly bonkers.
> DOCTOR: (to console) It's okay, it's okay.
> CLARA: You're like one of those guys who can't go out with a girl unless his mother approves.
> DOCTOR: It's important to me you get along. I could leave you two alone together.
> CLARA: Now you're creeping me out. ("Journey to the Centre of the TARDIS")

TARDIS Key

The First Doctor and Ian have a compass that can locate the TARDIS (*The Chase*) and the Third Doctor has a wristwatch version of the device in *Spearhead from Space*. Still, keys are more standard.

The key "unlocks" the double-curtain trimonic barrier that protects the Main Doors. It is isomorphic and apparently will only work for its designated user. Some versions resemble a simple earth key while others have the Seal of Gallifrey or Constellation of Kasterborus inscribed on the back. The keys contain perception filters, which can protect their holders and biologically link with their users – a metabolism detector on the lock keeps out those who haven't been authorized. Nevertheless, on a few occasions, strangers successfully use the Doctor's key (*The War Machines*, *Doctor*

Who Movie, "Blink").

The TARDIS can also be locked from the inside, preventing even authorized individuals from using the key and entering (*The Dalek Invasion of Earth*, "Utopia"). The Tenth Doctor has a remote lock much like a car's, which even makes the roof light flash and an alarm chirp (*The End of Time*). The Twelfth Doctor keeps seven keys hidden around the TARDIS ("Dark Water").

Other Time Machines

Other time travel devices appear through the series. Magnus Greel in *The Talons of Weng-Chiang* has a primitive machine that can prove fatal. The Daleks try to gain control of the Solar System with a time-accelerating "Time Destructor" in *The Daleks' Master Plan* and they also develop a "time corridor." The Time/Space Visualizer allows the First Doctor to watch events in history (*The Space Museum*, *The Chase*).

The Time Lords give the Fourth Doctor a time ring so he can escape danger in *Genesis of the Daleks*. The Time Lords also have a "time scoop" which can gather individuals – even different incarnations of the Doctor at once. It appears in "The Five Doctors" and the novel *The Eight Doctors* and the final chapter of the *Gallifrey* audio series. There's a time corridor in *Timelash*. The Hand of Omega can collapse a star into a black hole or destroy entire systems, though it can also be used for time travel – the Seventh Doctor struggles to stop this device in *Remembrance of the Daleks*.

A rough and dirty wrist-mounted vortex manipulator allows short "hops" through the Time Vortex. The Family of Blood has one. Captain Jack Harkness uses one often – the Doctor disables it at the end of "Last of the Time Lords" and "Journey's End" but Jack continues to repair it. The Doctor disdainfully compares the "space hopper" vortex manipulator to his "sports car" TARDIS. In "The Pandorica Opens," River Song buys one from a black market dealer in order to meet the Doctor. The Doctor uses it himself in to travel back in time and have the Auton copy of Rory Williams free him from the Pandorica. He returns it to River at episode end. She uses it, even in prison, in the "First Night" and "Last Night" minisodes and on other adventures. By 2013, Jack Harkness' vortex manipulator has fallen into UNIT's possession ("The Day of the Doctor,") and Clara uses it to travel back to 1562 and reunite with the Doctor.

On *Torchwood*, "Captain Jack Harkness" and "End of Days" offer a Rift Manipulator at the Torchwood Hub, which can complete minor time travel. It somewhat resembles the central column of the TARDIS console. It is also used in the episode "The Stolen Earth" to boost a distress call to the Doctor and then in "Journey's End" to help the TARDIS drag the Earth back into its regular orbit.

There's also a transmat, or transporter, used in *The Seeds of Death, The Ark in Space, Revenge of the Cybermen, The Armageddon Factor, The Five Doctors, Mawdryn Undead, The Twin Dilemma, Remembrance of the Daleks*, "Bad Wolf," and "Journey's End," among others

Spinoffs

An Adventure in Space and Time

This touching homage to the creators of the amazing cult show offers a delightful treat for fans, bookending the series with its beginning before the 50th anniversary special.

In the docu-drama, producer Verity Lambert get her start, learning beside the terribly young director Waris Hussein as they both fight the white male dominated BBC. Watching Verity defend the Daleks' existence is a special treat. As she uses expressions like "Brave heart," or Hartnell asks "Doctor Who?" the program nods to its many episodes and in-jokes. The music turns menacing for the Daleks but also shows the creation of the theme song (unchanged in 50 years!) and the sound effects.

Of course, there's the traditional period music and costumes placing the show firmly in the 60s. The first woman in space and the Kennedy assassination appear side by side. Viewers get to visit a world of taping where four takes was considered far too much effort, with no budget and none of today's tech.

Watching William Hartnell bond with his granddaughter through his relationship with his fictional granddaughter and his science fiction adventures is a delight. Of course this is framed partly as his struggle, his adventure to grow into a science fiction legend. At the same time, the series itself gains fannish status as kids on the bus start chanting "Exterminate!" and the first fan magazines and merchandising appear as the show begins to show what a success it can be. When a new

THE CATCHUP GUIDE TO DOCTOR WHO

producer joins, it's lovely to see Hartnell being fannish, insisting that the proper buttons must do the proper jobs. With something on Verity's cheek and the toasting photo of actors there's a lovely cycle back to the beginning as the show tells a good story with artistry and heart as well as all its nods to fans. The device of dialing the TARDIS to achieve flashbacks and flashforwards is charming for fans as well. Of course so many script moments from entering the TARDIS to the Daleks to the Doctor's farewell to Susan are refilmed, along with the making of parts of the episode. As the show ends with a few actual actors and contributors, this delightful docu-drama takes its place in history...and the history of time itself.

Big Finish Audio Productions

From 1999 on, Big Finish has produced many Doctor Who Audio Adventures, in which many of the original actors appear. Approximately thirteen appear per year, one every month with two in September. Various series have featured *The Fourth Doctor, The Eighth Doctor, Early Adventures,* and spinoffs in the Dalek Empire or UNIT. *I, Davros* follows the supervillain, while some companions, from Sarah Jane Smith to original audio characters Iris Wildthyme and Charlotte Pollard have independent adventures.

Comics

Terry Nation, who had joint rights with the BBC to the Daleks, created a regular Dalek comic strip in *TV Century 21* magazine in 1964. While the Doctor didn't appear, the Daleks battled many races.

The *Doctor Who* comic strip, published in *TV Comic* in 1964 continues through today as the longest running TV-related comic strip (Kistler 46). In 1979, the strip moved to *Doctor Who Weekly* (today *Doctor Who Magazine*), tied to currently continuity and the current Doctor. Just before the reboot, Davies offered to let the magazine do the regeneration scene from the Eighth Doctor to the Ninth, but they preferred not to lose the Doctor's then-traveling companion Destrii, so they simply showed her and Eight walking into the sunset. Additional comics appear in the *Doctor Who Annuals*.

Curse of the Fatal Death
This is a parody starring Rowan Atkinson and several other famous actors (Richard E Grant, Jim Broadbent, Hugh Grant, and Joanna Lumley) as the Doctor. It also contains the only female incarnation of the Doctor. It was written in 1999 by Steven Moffat and played on BBC as part of a charity drive for Children in Need.

Dimensions in Time
Dimensions in Time is a Children in Need charity crossover between *Doctor Who* and the soap opera *EastEnders* that ran in 1993 for the Thirtieth Anniversary, though the show was then off the air. It features several of the *EastEnders* stars of the time along with Doctors Three through Seven and a large ensemble of companions. Producer John Nathan-Turner explains:

> The TARDIS arrives in London and gets embroiled with characters from *Eastenders* in a two-part mini-adventure in 3D, a very exciting technology that I don't think we've seen the end of. The story has all five living Doctors, twelve companions, a multitude of characters from *Eastenders*, and a multitude of monsters, something like twenty different monsters. (*Doctor Who Interviews*)

The Rani (in her third and final television appearance) has already captured Doctors One and Two, and seeks to capture the others, locking them in a time loop. She cycles through the Doctor's lives until all his incarnations wander London, mismatched with the wrong companions, meeting characters from EastEnders. They find themselves in 1973, 1993, and 2013. The Rani also releases creatures from a Cyberman to a Sea Devil from her menagerie. The Fourth Doctor warns:

171

Mayday! Mayday! This is an urgent message for all the Doctors. It's vitally important that you listen carefully to me for once. Our whole existence is being threatened by a renegade Time Lord known only as the Rani! She hates me. She even hates children! Two of my earlier selves have already been snared in her vicious trap. The grumpy one and the flautist, do you remember? She wants to put us out of action, lock us away in a dreary backwater of London's East End, trapped in a time-loop in perpetuity. Her evil is all around us! I can hear the heartbeat of a killer. She's out there somewhere. We must be on our guard and we must stop her before she destroys all of my other selves! Oh... Good luck, my dears!

At last, the Doctors defeat the Rani and trap her in her own device.

Direct to Video

After cancelation, Bill Baggs created the production company BBV and made straight-to-video adventures basically in the Whoniverse. 1991 had the first. The "Stranger," Colin Baker was an alien living on earth, assisted by "Miss Brown," Nicola Bryant (Peri). In 1993, *The Airzone Solution* was a mainstream drama starring the actors who played Three, Five, Six, and Seven, along with Nicola Bryant and Sophie Aldred. Gatiss wrote some episodes for the series called P.R.O.B.E, starring Caroline John as Liz Shaw. Nicholas Briggs also wrote some Auton stories.

1994 offered *Shakedown: Return of the Sontarans* from Dreamwatch Media and Reeltime Pictures, with a Sontaran-Rutan battle. Reeltime also produced *Downtime* and *Daemos Rising*, featuring the Brigadier and his daughter, companion Victoria, and the Great Intelligence. In the Tenth Doctor's era, he and Martha appear in the animated adventures *The Infinite Quest* and *Dreamtime*, available on DVD.

Direct to Web

Scream of the Shalka was a flash-animated *Doctor Who* serial that offered Richard E Grant as the Ninth Doctor in 2003.

However, the 2006 reboot canceled out this non-canon production. An online short story, *The Feast of the Stone* by Cavan Scott and Mark Wright, also features this Doctor. (Richard E Grant went on to play the Great Intelligence in Series Seven).

During the times of Doctors Ten and Eleven, numerous minisodes appeared on Youtube, often produced to benefit Comic Relief and offering extra tiny adventures or missing scenes in the Doctors adventures. All had Tennant or Smith as the Doctor, and some had other characters, from companions to Ood to Albert Einstein. The Fiftieth anniversary had two minisodes: "The Last Day" following Arcadia's fall and "The Night of the Doctor," following the transformation of Eight into the War Doctor. There was also the half hour special "The Five-ish Doctors" in which Five, Six and Seven's actors attempt to appear in the special.

K9

In the time of the Fourth Doctor, *K9 and Company* (starring the beloved dog and Sarah Jane) had a pilot made but never succeeded as a series. Nonetheless, it appears treated as canon, as Sarah Jane has a K9 in *The Five Doctors,* "School Reunion" and her own subsequent series.

Meanwhile, *K-9* is an Australian series for adolescents focusing on the robot dog, mixing computer animation and live action. A season of thirty-minute episodes aired in 2009 and 2010 on Network Ten in Australia, and on Disney XD in Europe. In near-future London, 14-year old Starkey and Jorjie, alongside a Professor Gryffen with his Space-Time Manipulator, and 15-year-old Darius, his errand boy, protect the earth from the villainous reptilian warrior Jixen and other threats. This series was the reason the character had limited appearances on *The Sarah Jane Adventures.*

Novels

In 1964, David Whitaker adapted the original Dalek episode into the first *Doctor Who* novelization, *Doctor Who and the*

Daleks (originally titled *Doctor Who in an Exciting Adventure with the Daleks*). *Doctor Who in an Exciting Adventure with the Daleks* and *Doctor Who and the Crusaders*, adapted by David Whitaker, and *Doctor Who and the Zarbi*, adapted by Bill Strutton, were published as hardbacks in the sixties. In 1973, Target Books reprinted these three titles to begin their new series, and adapted all the episodes into book versions. Before home video, these novelizations were the only way to relive the stories as well as enjoy the missing episodes. Original novels joined them, beginning with *Doctor Who and the Auton Invasion* by Terrance Dicks in 1974. A long series followed.

Virgin Missing Adventures (1994-1997) revisited past Doctors. From 1991-1997, the Virgin New Adventures followed the Seventh Doctor as he continued traveling after the series went off the air. His companion was Bernice Summerfield, who had adventures in the books without him from 1997-1999. (In 1996, the BBC decided to do their own line of novels with the new Eighth Doctor and a series of new companions, beginning with Sam Jones.) The BBC also produced a Past Doctor Adventures line of books.

The New Series Adventures follow the modern Doctors, from Nine on, and are published by BBC Books. Their audio book editions are narrated by many Who stars including David Tennant.

The Decalogs are three collections of original Doctor Who short stories, all of which were written to fit in with NA and MA continuity. There is another series of novellas from Telos Publishing. *Short Trips* are collections of original short stories. There are also original *Torchwood* novels, *Sarah Jane Adventures* novelizations and *The Adventures of K9* (Sparrow, 1980). Stores also crowd with RPG books, released scripts, and nonfiction, dating from the beginning to current times. *The Doctor Who Reference Guide* (Drwhoguide.com) has a detailed list.

Theatrical Movies and Plays

In 1965, the full color theater film *Dr. Who and the Daleks* appeared, loosely adapted from the first Dalek episode and considered outside canon. Peter Cushing plays the Doctor with a reimagined Barbara, Susan, and Ian. *Daleks Invasion Earth: 2150 A.D.* soon followed the next year. Susan and new companion Louise accompany him, along with policeman Tom Campbell, played by Bernard Cribbins, who plays Donna's grandfather Wilf in the new series. There have been several stage plays, including David Whitaker and Terry Nation's *The Curse of the Daleks* and *Doctor Who and the Seven Keys to Doomsday* by Terrance Dicks.

Torchwood
Captain Jack Harkness (John Barrowman) gains his own spinoff as he takes over the Torchwood Three team guarding the Cardiff Rift, seen in past and present in *Doctor Who* series one. Captain Jack declares the organization "outside the government and beyond the police" ("Everything Changes"), while alien threats appear almost every week. They operate in their offices, called the Hub, under the Roald Dahl plaza guarded by an invisible lift guarded by a perception filter presumably created during the events of "Boom Town."

There are four series – one and two take place during the Davies era, followed by the (surviving) team's guest appearance on *Doctor Who* for "The Stolen Earth"/"Journey's End." Next comes the five-part miniseries *Children of Earth* (2009) and the HBO ten-part *Miracle Day* (2011).

Captain Jack's new team is Suzie Costello (weapons specialist), Toshiko Sato (computer specialist) and Owen Harper (medical). These are played by Indira Varma, Naoko Mori, and Burn Gorman respectively. (Tosh appears earlier when she pretends to be a medical examiner in *Doctor Who*'s "Aliens of London.") Their fifth member, who joins to try to save his cyberwoman girlfriend, is Ianto Jones (Gareth David-Lloyd), often acting as operations specialist or even the team's butler. In episode one, "Everything Changes," Jack recruits police officer Gwen Cooper (Eve Myles). Her boyfriend Rhys is another main character, whom she marries in series two.

However, Suzie reveals herself as a murderess and Jack is forced to shoot her. In the series one finale, "End of Days" (2008), the Cardiff rift opens and the demon Abaddon invades. Jack defeats it with pure lifeforce, only to run off when he hears the TARDIS. He joins the Doctor and Martha for their own finale and returns to his team for Torchwood series two. He discovers Gwen has taken charge quite competently and that all the team feel betrayed by his sudden absence. Series two has Martha Jones guest-star, while Toshiko and Owen are killed in the pursuit of their duty ("Exit Wounds"). The three remaining team members help the Tenth Doctor restore the Earth to its original location ("The Stolen Earth"/"Journey's End").

In *Children of Earth* (2009), aliens called the 456 appear and demand a gift of children. The Torchwood team defies them and the British government turns on them, destroying the base and trying to kill them. Nonetheless, Captain Jack recruits Gwen and Rhys for the events of *Miracle Day* (2011). They travel between Britain and America investigating why death has stopped...an event that seems linked with Jack's sudden vulnerability. Jack himself has been recruited by the CIA and its new agent Rex Matheson. By series end, Rex shares in Jack's restored invulnerability, though the series does not return after this canon-changing event.

Sarah Jane Adventures

After the success of Sarah Jane Smith's return in "School Reunion" (Tenth Doctor), Russell T Davies created *The Sarah Jane Adventures* starring Elisabeth Sladen. This spin-off of mostly half-hour two part episodes is aimed at young viewers, as Sarah Jane defends earth alongside her adopted children and their neighborhood young people in Ealing. Doctors Ten and Eleven guest-star, along with the Brigadier and companion Jo Grant, all played by their original actors. K-9 appears in the pilot and in about half of series three and four. The show ran from 2007 to 2011, but unfortunately stopped abruptly with the lead actress's death.

Other characters include thirteen-year-old Maria Jackson (Yasmin Paige), fourteen-year-old Clyde Langer (Daniel Anthony), and Sarah Jane's adopted son Luke (Tommy Knight). After series one, Maria moves away and Rani Chandra and her parents, Haresh, and Gita (Anjli Mohindra, Ace Bhatti, and Mina Anwar) move in. In series five, a new child, Sky (Sinead Michael), is created for Sarah Jane. There is also Mr. Smith, Sarah Jane's alien computer. Besides Mr. Smith and K-9, Sarah Jane has several tools of alien tech. A scanner watch from the Tenth Doctor allows her to scan for alien life, while her sonic lipstick parallels his beloved screwdriver.

This delightful, sweet show sees Sarah Jane and her friends dealing with alien invasions of the school, evil corporations, and struggles to fit in and keep the alien invasions hidden. Recurring enemies include the Slitheen and Mrs. Wormwood, Luke's creator. There is also the Trickster, who gives people a sinister second chance at life. Several episodes show Sarah Jane revisiting past decisions and struggling with emotional crises, while others add to the Whoniverse lore, including revealing the fate of many human companions.

Final Questions

What are the Running Jokes?

- First comes the literal running joke, as characters spend much time running. Ten even wears trainers with his suits.
- People enter the TARDIS and say "it's bigger on the inside!"
- The banana-switched-for-gun gag actually started in the Eighth Doctor Adventures, before the Steven Moffat's episodes "The Empty Child" /"The Doctor Dances," "The Girl in the Fireplace," and "Let's Kill Hitler."
- People assume Gallifrey is in Ireland.
- The early Daleks were famously vulnerable to stairs – in "Dalek" this is no longer true.
- Aliens invade on Christmas every year, often with an absence of snow.
- Jaded humans, especially Londoners, ignore alien attacks and dismiss them as pranks. The Londoners at least remember the attacks enough to vacate the city in "Voyage of the Damned," anticipating another apocalypse.

ACE: But this is Earth, 1963. Well someone would've noticed, I'd have heard about it!
SEVENTH DOCTOR: Do you remember the Zygon gambit with the Loch Ness monster? Or the Yetis in the underground?
ACE: The what?

SEVENTH DOCTOR: Your species has the most amazing capacity for self-deception, matched only by its ingenuity when trying to destroy itself. (*Remembrance of the Daleks*)

There are a few exceptions – the locals of Cardiff know who Torchwood is. Awareness slowly grows as aliens invade London in the new series, over and over. But mostly, a Cyberman Invasion is meant with fans satirizing the "ghosts" on television or taking selfies with the soldiers in the square.

► Other jokes appear earlier in this book, as characters upon meeting the Doctor, ask, "Doctor Who?" Many episodes from "Time Crash" to "The Day of the Doctor" offer mentions of previous adventures.

Missing Episodes?
One of the holy grails of fandom is the *Doctor Who* missing episodes. To save space and reuse the expensive tapes, the BBC erased the master and sometimes only copies of many black and white episodes of the First and Second Doctors' six original seasons (along with many other old shows). Today, there are 26 incomplete *Doctor Who* serials missing 97 of 253 half-hour episodes. The rest have been recovered, mostly from overseas broadcasting companies. Fans at home recorded all the episodes in audio form, as video was not yet available. Today, there has been an effort to combine the audio with black and white cartoons based on promotional stills to recreate some of the missing sections for newly released DVDs. Nonetheless, many pieces of many episodes, including the first meetings of companions and Doctor, remain missing.

What's a Fixed Point in Time?
The history of the Doctor's universe is mutable until the point where the Doctor himself has observed it, either directly or indirectly. When he knows how the story must end, unless someone has already intervened to change it, he cannot alter it from its destined outcome – at least on a large

scale. Thus he insists he cannot prevent Pompeii exploding, but he does save one family. He cannot interfere with his own past (though this happens on occasion, especially when he rarely meets himself). Further, a fixed point requires that something *must* happen – if it does not, all of time can collapse. Nonetheless, if the Doctor must *appear* dead, this is not the same as a moment that requires his death.

The Female Doctor Question

When Tom Baker announced he was moving on, he stirred up the press conference when he added, "I wish the new Doctor, *whoever he or she is* the very best of luck. However, john Nathan-Turner retorted later, "there was never a chance then – nor do I think there ever will be – that the Doctor could be played by a woman. Absolutely not! (Haining 163).

"There has been no black, female, or working-class Doctor. All Doctors and companions have either been English or outer-space English (Until Nathan-Turner brought in an Australian actress to play Tegan)" (Tulloch and Alvarado 206). As such, there's a strong echo of class system – only white British males get to be the Doctor – women and people of color can only be his sidekicks. As another critic protests:

> After all, why haven't we had a female Doctor or a Doctor of color? Is it because s/he would lose all that power associated with being a white man? Does he need the power to strut through Earth history and the rest of the universe without a worry, the power to command and control, even if he doesn't use it? Are we fans as attracted to the Doctor's power as his companions are? (Stoker, Kindle Locations 2648-2651).

Many fans want a Doctor who "looks like them," so the issue resurfaces often – whenever the Doctor regenerates. Davies comments:

> While I think kids will not have a problem with [a female Doctor], I think fathers will have a problem with it because

they will then imagine they will have to describe sex changes to their children. I think fathers can describe sex changes to their children and I think they should and it's part of the world, but I think it would simply introduce genitalia into family viewing. You're not talking about actresses or style, you're talking about genitalia, and a lot of parents would get embarrassed. (Dowell, Kindle Locations 1028-1032).

Steven Moffat likewise hesitated. Nonetheless, in his tenure, hints began to accumulate. Moffat, in his parody, *The Curse of the Fatal Death*, has many actors play the Doctor, including Joanna Lumley. After Matt Smith regenerates, he touches his hair and wonders if he is a woman this time. Neil Gaiman's "The Doctor's Wife" mentions the Corsair, who had regenerated as male and female in turn. "Dark Water" sees the Master regenerate into "the Mistress," while in the sequel, "Death in Heaven," Clara claims she is the Doctor. The series is getting closer.

Whoniverse Episode Guide

First Doctor (William Hartnell) Seasons 1-3 1963-1965
001. An Unearthly Child
002. The Daleks
003. The Edge of Destruction
004. Marco Polo
005. The Keys of Marinus
006. The Aztecs
007. The Sensorites
008. The Reign of Terror
009. Planet of Giants
010. The Dalek Invasion of Earth
011. The Rescue
012. The Romans
013. The Web Planet
014. The Crusade
015. The Space Museum
016. The Chase
017. The Time Meddler
018. Galaxy 4
019. Mission to the Unknown
020. The Myth Makers
021. The Daleks' Master Plan
022. The Massacre of St Bartholomew's Eve
023. The Ark
024. The Celestial Toymaker
025. The Gunfighters
026. The Savages
027. The War Machines

028. The Smugglers
029. The Tenth Planet

Second Doctor (Patrick Troughton) Seasons 4-6 1966-1968
030. The Power of the Daleks
031. The Highlanders
032. The Underwater Menace
033. The Moonbase
034. The Macra Terror
035. The Faceless Ones
036. The Evil of the Daleks
037. The Tomb of the Cybermen
038. The Abominable Snowmen
039. The Ice Warriors
040. The Enemy of the World
041. The Web of Fear
042. Fury from the Deep
043. The Wheel in Space
044. The Dominators
045. The Mind Robber
046. The Invasion
047. The Krotons
048. The Seeds of Death
049. The Space Pirates
050. The War Games
051. Spearhead from Space
052. Doctor Who and the Silurians
053. The Ambassadors of Death
054. Inferno

Third Doctor (Jon Pertwee) Seasons 7-11 1970-1973
055. Terror of the Autons
056. The Mind of Evil
057. The Claws of Axos
058. Colony in Space
059. The Dæmons
060. Day of the Daleks
061. The Curse of Peladon

062. The Sea Devils
063. The Mutants
064. The Time Monster
065. The Three Doctors
066. Carnival of Monsters
067. Frontier in Space
068. Planet of the Daleks
069. The Green Death

Fourth Doctor (Tom Baker) Seasons 12-18 1974-1980
070. The Time Warrior
071. Invasion of the Dinosaurs
072. Death to the Daleks
073. The Monster of Peladon
074. Planet of the Spiders
075. Robot
076. The Ark in Space
077. The Sontaran Experiment
078. Genesis of the Daleks
079. Revenge of the Cybermen
080. Terror of the Zygons
081. Planet of Evil
082. Pyramids of Mars
083. The Android Invasion
084. The Brain of Morbius
085. The Seeds of Doom
086. The Masque of Mandragora
087. The Hand of Fear
088. The Deadly Assassin
089. The Face of Evil
090. The Robots of Death
091. The Talons of Weng-Chiang
092. Horror of Fang Rock
093. The Invisible Enemy
094. Image of the Fendahl
095. The Sun Makers
096. Underworld
097. The Invasion of Time

098. The Ribos Operation
099. The Pirate Planet
100. The Stones of Blood
101. The Androids of Tara
102. The Power of Kroll
103. The Armageddon Factor
104. Destiny of the Daleks
105. City of Death
106. The Creature from the Pit
107. Nightmare of Eden
108. The Horns of Nimon
109. The Leisure Hive
110. Meglos
111. Full Circle
112. State of Decay
113. Warriors' Gate
114. The Keeper Of Traken
115. Logopolis

Fifth Doctor (Peter Davison) Seasons 19-21 1982-1984
116. Castrovalva
117. Four to Doomsday
118. Kinda
119. The Visitation
120. Black Orchid
121. Earthshock
122. Time-Flight
123. Arc of Infinity
124. Snakedance
125. Mawdryn Undead
126. Terminus
127. Enlightenment
128. The King's Demons
129. The Five Doctors
130. Warriors of the Deep
131. The Awakening
132. Frontios
133. Resurrection of the Daleks

134. Planet of Fire
135. The Caves of Androzani

Sixth Doctor (Colin Baker) Seasons 22-23 1985-1986
136. The Twin Dilemma
137. Attack of the Cybermen
138. Vengeance On Varos
139. The Mark of The Rani
140. The Two Doctors
141. Timelash
142. Revelation of the Daleks
143. The Trial of a Time Lord
         The Trial of a Time Lord: The Mysterious Planet
         The Trial of a Time Lord: Mindwarp
         The Trial of a Time Lord: Terror of the Vervoids
         The Trial of a Time Lord: The Ultimate Foe

Seventh Doctor (Sylvester McCoy) Seasons 24-26 1987-1989
144. Time and the Rani
145. Paradise Towers
146. Delta and the Bannermen
147. Dragonfire
148. Remembrance of the Daleks
149. The Happiness Patrol
150. Silver Nemesis
151. The Greatest Show in the Galaxy
152. Battlefield
153. Ghost Light
154. The Curse of Fenric
155. Survival

Eighth Doctor (Paul McGann) 1996
156 Doctor Who Television Movie (The Enemy Within)

Old Numbering	New Who	Modern Numbering
Series 1	**Ninth Doctor and**	
2005	**Rose Tyler**	
157	Rose	1.1
158	The End of the World	1.2
159	The Unquiet Dead	1.3
160	Aliens of London	1.4
	World War Three	1.5
161	Dalek	1.6
162	The Long Game	1.7
163	Father's Day	1.8
164	The Empty Child	1.9
	The Doctor Dances	1.10
165	Boom Town	1.11
166	Bad Wolf	1.12
	The Parting of the Ways	1.13
	Children in Need	Special
Series 2	**Tenth Doctor and**	
2006	**Rose Tyler**	
167	The Christmas Invasion	Christmas Special
168	New Earth	2.1
169	Tooth and Claw	2.2
170	School Reunion	2.3
171	The Girl in the Fireplace	2.4
172	Rise of the Cybermen	2.5
	The Age of Steel	2.6
173	The Idiot's Lantern	2.7
174	The Impossible Planet	2.8
	The Satan Pit	2.9
175	Love & Monsters	2.1
176	Fear Her	2.11
177	Army of Ghosts	2.12
	Doomsday	2.13

Series 3	Tenth Doctor and	
2007	Martha Jones	
178	The Runaway Bride	Christmas Special
179	Smith and Jones	3.1
180	The Shakespeare Code	3.2
181	Gridlock	3.3
182	Daleks in Manhattan	3.4
	Evolution of the Daleks	3.5
183	Lazarus Experiment	3.6
184	42	3.7
185	Human Nature	3.8
	The Family of Blood	3.9
186	Blink	3.1
187	Utopia	3.11
	The Sound of Drums	3.12
	Last of the Time Lords	3.13
	Time Crash	Short
	Voyage of the Damned	Christmas Special
Series 4	Tenth Doctor and	
2008	Donna Noble	
189	Partners in Crime	4.1
190	The Fires of Pompeii	4.3
191	Planet of the Ood	4.2
192	The Sontaran Stratagem	4.4
	The Poison Sky	4.5
193	The Doctor's Daughter	4.6
194	The Unicorn and the Wasp	4.7
195	Silence in the Library	4.9
	Forest of the Dead	4.1
196	Midnight	4.8
197	Turn Left	4.11
198	The Stolen Earth	4.12
199	Journey's End	4.13
200	The Next Doctor	Christmas Special

190

191

Series 8	Twelfth Doctor, Clara	
2014	**Oswald**	
242	Deep Breath	8.1
243	Into the Dalek	8.2
244	Robot of Sherwood	8.3
245	Listen	8.4
246	Time Heist	8.5
247	The Caretaker	8.6
248	Kill the Moon	8.7
249	Mummy on the Orient Express	8.8
250	Flatline	8.9
251	In the Forest of the Night	8.10
252	Dark Water	8.11
253	Death in Heaven	8.12
254	Last Christmas	Christmas Special

Torchwood
Series 1 2006

Everything Changes	1.1
Day One	1.2
Ghost Machine	1.3
Cyberwoman	1.4
Small Worlds	1.5
Countrycide	1.6
Greeks Bearing Gifts	1.7
They Keep Killing Suzie	1.8
Random Shoes	1.9
Out of Time	1.10
Combat	1.11
Captain Jack Harkness	1.12
End of Days	1.13

Series 2 2008

Kiss Kiss, Bang Bang	2.1
Sleeper	2.2
To the Last Man	2.3

Meat	2.4
Adam	2.5
Reset	2.6
Dead Man Walking	2.7
A Day in the Death	2.8
Something Borrowed	2.9
From Out of the Rain	2.10
Adrift	2.11
Fragments	2.12
Exit Wounds	2.13

2009 Miniseries   5 parts
Children of Earth

2011 Miniseries   10 parts
Miracle Day

The Sarah Jane Adventures
Series 1 2007

Invasion of the Bane	New Year's Special
Revenge of the Slitheen	1.1-1.2
Eye of the Gorgon	1.3-1.4
Warriors of Kudlak	1.5-1.6
Whatever Happened to Sarah Jane?	1.7-1.8
The Lost Boy	1.9-1.10

Series 2 2008

The Last Sontaran	2.1-2.2
The Day of the Clown	2.3-2.4
Secrets of the Stars	2.5-2.6
The Mark of the Berserker	2.7-2.8
The Temptation of Sarah Jane Smith	2.9-2.10
Enemy of the Bane	2.11-2.12

Series 3 2009

From Raxacoricofallapatorius with Love	Short
Prisoner of the Judoon	3.1-3.2
The Mad Woman in the Attic	3.3-3.4
The Wedding of Sarah Jane Smith	3.5-3.6
The Eternity Trap	3.7-3.8
Mona Lisa's Revenge	3.9-3.10
The Gift	3.11-3.12

Series 4 2010

The Nightmare Man	4.1-4.2
The Vault of Secrets	4.3-4.4
Death of the Doctor	4.5-4.6
The Empty Planet	4.7-4.8
Lost in Time	4.9-4.10
Goodbye, Sarah Jane Smith	4.11-4.12

Series 5 2011

Sky	5.1-5.2
The Curse of Clyde Langer	5.3-5.4
The Man Who Never Was	5.5-5.6

Additional Specials

Dr. Who and the Daleks (Peter Cushing as the Doctor) 1965

Daleks' Invasion of Earth 2150 A.D (Peter Cushing as the Doctor) 1966

Shada, Unfinished episode released later on DVD (Fourth Doctor and Romana) 1979

K-9 and Company: A Girl's Best Friend (Sarah Jane Smith) 1981

Dimensions in Time, Crossover with EastEnders (Jon Pertwee, Tom Baker, Peter Davison, Colin Baker and Sylvester McCoy as the Doctor plus many of the companions) 1993

Doctor Who and the Curse of Fatal Death (Rowan Atkinson, Joanna Lumley, Hugh Grant, Richard E. Grant and Jim Broadbent as the Doctor) 1999

Death Comes to Time, webcast (Seventh Doctor and Ace) 2001

Real Time, webcast (Sixth Doctor) 2002

Scream of the Shalka (Richard Grant as the Doctor) 2003

Attack of the Graske (Tenth Doctor and Rose short) 2005

TARDISodes, one minute introductions to each Series Two episode (Tenth Doctor and Rose), 2006

The Infinite Quest (Tenth Doctor and Martha) 2007

Music of the Spheres (Tenth Doctor short) 2008

Dreamland (Tenth Doctor) 2009

K-9, animated show (John Leeson as K-9) 2009-2010.

"500 miles" and "The Ballad of Russell and Julie," music videos (Tenth Doctor and cast and crew) 2010

Death is the Only Answer (Eleventh Doctor short) 2011

The Doctor's Clothes (Eleventh Doctor short) 2011

Good as Gold (Eleventh Doctor short) 2012

The Night of the Doctor (Eighth Doctor short) 2013

An Adventure in Space and Time (Docu-drama) 2013

List of Doctors and Companions

The Doctor (s):
1. William Hartnell 1963 – 1966
2. Patrick Troughton 1966 – 1969
3. Jon Pertwee 1970 – 1974
4. Tom Baker 1974 – 1981
5. Peter Davison 1981 – 1984
6. Colin Baker 1984 – 1986
7. Sylvester McCoy 1987 – 1989
8. Paul McGann (1996 movie + audio productions)
?. John Hurt 2013
9. Christopher Eccleston 2005
10. David Tennant 2005 – 2009
11.Matt Smith 2010 – 2013
12. Peter Capaldi 2014 –

Principal Companions:
Carole Ann Ford as Susan Foreman 1963 – 1964
Jacqueline Hill as Barbara Wright 1963 – 1965
William Russell as Ian Chesterton 1963 – 1965
Maureen O'Brien as Vicki 1965
Adrienne Hill as Katarina 1965
Jean Marsh as Sara Kingdom 1965
Peter Purves as Steven Taylor 1965 – 1966
Jackie Lane as Dodo (Dorothea) Chaplet 1966
Anneka Wills as Polly 1966 – 1967
Michael Craze as Ben Jackson 1966 – 1967

Fraser Hines as Jamie McCrimmon 1966 – 1969
Deborah Watling as Victoria Waterfield 1967 – 1968
Wendy Padbury as Zoe Heriot 1968 – 1969
Caroline John as Liz Shaw 1970
Katy Manning as Jo Grant 1971 – 1973
Elisabeth Sladen as Sarah Jane Smith 1973 – 1976
Ian Marter as Surgeon Lt Harry Sullivan, RN 1974 – 1975
Louise Jameson as Leela 1977 – 1978
Mary Tamm as Romana 1978
Lalla Ward as Romana 1979 – 1981
Matthew Waterhouse as Adric 1980 – 1982
Sarah Sutton as Nyssa 1981 – 1983
Janet Fielding as Tegan Jovanka 1981 – 1984
Mark Strickson as Turlough 1983 – 1984
Nicola Bryant as Peri Brown 1984 – 1986
Bonnie Langford as Melanie Bush 1986 – 1987
Sophie Aldred as Ace 1987 – 1989
Daphne Ashbrook as Doctor Grace Holloway 1996
Billie Piper as Rose Tyler 2005 – 2006
Bruno Langley as Adam Mitchell 2005
John Barrowman as Jack Harkness 2005
Noel Clarke as Mickey Smith 2006
Freema Ageyman as Martha Jones 2007
Catherine Tate as Donna Noble 2008
Karen Gillan as Amy Pond 2010 – 2012
Arthur Darvill as Rory Williams 2010 – 2012
Alex Kingston as River Song 2010 -2013
Jenna-Louise Coleman as Clara Oswin Oswald 2012 – 2014

Glossary of Terms and Abbreviations

Arc, arc stories: A storyline that lasts through multiple episodes, like River and the Doctor's backwards romance or the crack in Amy's wall, shown in each episode of Series Five.

BBC: Station that distributes *Doctor Who,* classic and modern. BBC publishing also produces much supplementary nonfiction and published the Eighth Doctor Adventures and Past Doctor Adventures.

Big Finish Productions: Publisher of audio adventures starring many of the original *Who* actors from 1999 onwards.

Blog: Short for "Weblog," an online journal that may discuss pop culture.

Canon: This term refers to material designated "official" or "sanctioned by the author or producer" contrasted with other authors' contributions to a franchise (The *Star Wars* movies, for instance, are considered canon; the novels and comics are not).

Classic *Doctor Who* (*Old Who*): The show lasted from 1963 to 1989, with a television movie in 1996. It included the first eight Doctors, the TARDIS, and short multi-part adventures. The first two Doctors' eras were filmed in black and white, and a number of these episodes are missing.

Companions: *New Who* Companions of the Ninth and Tenth Doctor include Rose Tyler, Jack Harkness, Mickey Smith, Martha Jones, and Donna Noble. Companions of the Eleventh include Amy Pond, Rory Williams, River Song, and Clara Oswald.

Conventions: Fannish gatherings. Comic-Con in San Diego is the largest and most famous, while there are Comic-Con branches appearing in many other locations. Gallifrey One and Chicago TARDIS are top *Who* conventions.

Cosplay: Short for "costume play." Wearing costumes and occasionally acting them out.

Crossover fiction: Fan fiction, fan art, etc. that combines more than one series, such as *Doctor Who* and *Star Trek*.

Davies: Russell T Davies was responsible for reviving the show and remained in charge from 2005-2009 during the Tenth and Eleventh Doctors' eras, series 1-4.

Doctor Who Magazine: The most well-known fan production, running from 1979 through now.

Doctor: Considered the same character, though played by different actors, with different personalities. His name is unknown.

DVDs: Most *Doctor Who* episodes have been released this way, including *New Who, Old Who* individual episodes, and sometimes the only remaining fragments of missing episodes as part of a larger themed collection. Cartoon episodes and parodies are also available on DVD.

Expanded Universe: Refers to the novels, comics, audio adventures, games, parodies, and other "semicanon" or "noncanon" material, in contrast with the television show.

Fan art: Noncommercial art based on the series and frequently posted on the web to share with other fans.

Fan communities: These could refer to fan groups that meet in person or on the web.

Fan fiction: Also called "fanfic." Noncommercial fiction based on the series and generally posted on the web.

Fan groups: Social groups (usually organized by region and meeting in person) devoted to activities and discussion of the series.

Fan service: Scenes intended to please longtime fans rather than tell a strong story.

Fan sites: Websites devoted to the show often containing news, encyclopedias, discussion boards, or fan art and fan fiction. The TARDIS Data Core is the largest repository of information, while *Doctor Who Online, Doctor Who.com, WhovianNet,* many forums and Facebook pages fill the web.

IDW Comics: American producer of *Doctor Who* comic books and graphic novels

K-9: Beloved robot dog of the Fourth Doctor era, also seen in "School Reunion" and some of *The Sarah Jane Adventures.* The attempted spinoff *K-9 and Company* only had a pilot, and the Australian show *K9* appears to have only lasted briefly.

Minisode: Episode continuations (usually only five minutes) that were filmed for Children in Need or various promotional specials and are generally included on the DVDs. These were particularly made in the Tenth and Eleventh Doctor eras to take advantage of new media. Most are available on YouTube.

Missing Episodes: Many episodes from the black and white era were discarded. Only in 1978 was an effort made to collect them by the BBC Film and Videotape Library. In 1983, a total of 134 episodes (sections of original 4-parters or other multipart serials) were missing, believed lost, and by the 50th anniversary in 2013, 97 episodes were still undiscovered. A few have been recreated using audio recordings, original promotional stills, and cartoons.

MMO: A Massively Multiplayer Online game, which can also function as a fannish community

Moffat: Steven Moffat wrote some episodes during Davies' reign, and then took over the show with the Eleventh Doctor.

New Doctor Who (*New Who*): The 2005 show is in a modern one-hour format, with Christmas specials, minisodes, and other experimental forms as well. It has heavy story arcs through each year.

New Series Adventures: *New Who* books aimed at kids

Novelizations: Generally an adaptation of the same story in a novel medium – the novelization of the popular episode "Genesis of the Daleks" contains extra material, but is basically the same adventure.

NPC: A Non Player Character in a computer game – someone written in who functions as part of the story.

Podcasts: A form of internet radio, with many Who fansites.

Puffin: For the Fiftieth Anniversary, Puffin ebooks is releasing eleven authors' short stories, one for each Doctor.

Retcon: Retroactive Continuity Change, contradicting a fact that was previously established. *Torchwood* humorously invents the drug "retcon" to aid them in this practice.

RPG: Role Playing Game such as *Dungeons and Dragons*. There are *Doctor Who* versions.

The Sarah Jane Adventures (SJA): A 2007 spin-off based off the *Doctor Who* episode "School Reunion," in which beloved companion Sarah Jane Smith (Elisabeth Sladen) from original *Who* returns but prefers to adventure on earth. It's a children's show as she outwits aliens with the help of her adopted teen children and their neighborhood friends. The show was unfortunately canceled with the actress's death in 2011.

Season: In the US this refers to a year of a show. In the UK, this term used to be used (and thus, is used to refer to, say, season 19 of the old show) but no longer is.

Series: The current name for a year of a show in the UK. Thus, *New Who* is divided into series 1 through 7. The show went from Season 26 to a television movie to Series 1, technically speaking.

Shipping: Writing, creating art, etc. devoted to a particular relationship between characters.

Ships: Short for relationships; a popular term used in fan fiction.

Slash: Refers to romantic homosexual relationships not evident in the series (such as Harry Potter and Draco Malfoy, or the Doctor and the Master). This is a popular genre of fanfiction.

Speculative Fiction: An all-encompassing name for science fiction and fantasy.

Target: Publishers of the original novelizations and *The Companions of Doctor Who*.

Torchwood (TW): A 2006 spin-off from *Doctor Who*, managed by Davies. It follows the adventures of the Torchwood 3 team in Cardiff as they hunt aliens. It had two years, then the five-part miniseries *Torchwood: Children of Earth*, then a year on Starz as *Torchwood: Miracle Day* in 2011. All four series starred John Barrowman as Captain Jack Harkness and Eve Myles as Gwen Cooper.

Transcripts: Written form of the audio/visual recordings. A full fan-created set of all fifty years of episodes is available at *Chrissie's Transcripts Site* at Chakoteya.net.

Trock Rock: Short for Time Lord Rock. Independent bands write songs about *Doctor Who* and its characters.

Virgin New Adventures: Continuing novels of the Seventh and Eighth Doctors published after the series ended in 1989.

Whoniverse: Fannish name for the fictional universe containing old and new *Doctor Who, Sarah Jane Adventures, Torchwood*, and often the Expanded Universe stories and fanfiction.

Youtube: www.YouTube.com. Most of the minisodes, and some cast and crew interviews are available free on Youtube, along with the David Tennant music videos.

Works Cited

Primary Sources

Doctor Who: The Complete Eighth Series (2014; BBC Home Entertainment, 2014), DVD.

Doctor Who: The Complete Fifth Series (2010; BBC Home Entertainment, 2010), DVD.

Doctor Who: The Complete First Series (2005; BBC Home Entertainment, 2005), DVD.

Doctor Who: The Complete Fourth Series (2008; BBC Home Entertainment, 2008), DVD.

Doctor Who: The Complete Second Series (2006; BBC Home Entertainment, 2006), DVD.

Doctor Who: The Complete Seventh Series (2013; BBC Home Entertainment, 2012), DVD.

Doctor Who: The Complete Sixth Series (2011; BBC Home Entertainment, 2011), DVD.

Doctor Who: The Complete Third Series (2007; BBC Home Entertainment, 2007), DVD.

Doctor Who original episodes (various). DVD.

The Sarah Jane Adventures: The Complete Fifth Season (BBC Home Entertainment, 2012), DVD.

The Sarah Jane Adventures: The Complete First Season (2008; BBC Home Entertainment, 2008), DVD.

The Sarah Jane Adventures: The Complete Fourth Season (2011; BBC Home Entertainment, 2011), DVD.

The Sarah Jane Adventures: The Complete Second Season (2009; BBC Home Entertainment, 2009), DVD.

The Sarah Jane Adventures: The Complete Third Season (2010; BBC Home Entertainment, 2010), DVD.

Torchwood: The Complete First Season (2008; BBC Home
Entertainment, 2007), DVD.
Torchwood: The Complete Second Season (2008; BBC Home
Entertainment, 2008), DVD.

Secondary Sources
Anders, Charlie Jane. "The River Song Scene That Was "Too
Naughty for *Doctor Who.*" *io9* 7 Oct 2011.
http://io9.com/5847768/the-river-song-scene-that-was-
too-naughty-for-doctor-who
Belam, Martin, Ed. *Who's Who? The Resurrection of the Doctor
(Guardian Shorts)*. UK: Guardian Books, 2011. Kindle
Edition.
Britton, Piers D. *TARDISbound*. New York: IB Tauris, 2011.
Burdge, Anthony *The Mythological Dimensions of Doctor Who*.
MythInk Books. Kindle Edition.
Burke, Jessica. "Doctor Who and the Valkyrie Tradition, Part
2: Goddesses, Battle-demons, Witches, & Wives" Burdge
140-182.
Butler, David, ed. *Time and Relative Dissertations in Space: Critical
Perspectives on Doctor Who*. Manchester: University of
Manchester Press, 2007.
Caron, Nathalie. "Steven Moffat Explains Why He'll Never
Bring Back The Rani on Who." *Blastr* 24 Aug 2012.
www.blastr.com/2012/08/steven_moffat_explains_wh.p
hp
--. "Steven Moffat Explains Why He Had to Bring Back the
Zygons for Who's 50th." *Blastr* 22 Oct 2013.
http://www.blastr.com/2013-10-22/steven-moffat-
explains-why-he-had-bring-back-zygons-
who%E2%80%99s-50th
Craig, Olga. "Penelope Wilton: An Actress Who Epitomises
All Things Quintessentially English." *The Daily Telegraph*
15 Nov 2008.
http://www.telegraph.co.uk/news/celebritynews/34652
47/Penelope-Wilton-an-actress-who-epitomises-all-
things-quintessentially-English.html

Davies, Russell T and Cook, Benjamin. *The Writer's Tale*. UK: Random House, 2008.

Davies, Russell T. and Benjamin Cook. *Doctor Who: The Writer's Tale: The Final Chapter*. UK: Random House, 2013.

Dipaolo, Marc Edward. "Political Satire and British-American Relations in Five Decades of Doctor Who." *Journal of Popular Culture* 43, no. 5 (October 2010): 964-987. *Academic Search Complete*.

Doctor Who Confidential. "Blink." 2007-06-09. BBC.

"Doctor Who Greatest Moments: The Companions." BBC. 2009.

Doctor Who Interviews. http://drwhointerviews.wordpress.com.

Dowell, Ben. "Russell T Davies to Step Down as Doctor Who 'Show-runner'." *The Guardian* Monday 7 July 2008. Belam.

Frankel, Valerie Estelle. *Doctor Who and the Hero's Journey*. USA: Thought Catalog 2013.

--. *Doctor Who - The What, Where, and How: A Fannish Guide to the TARDIS-Sized Pop Culture Jam*. USA: LitCrit Press, 2013.

Gaiman, Neil. "Neil Gaiman Q&A Highlights" 16 May 2011 *Doctor Who TV*.

Gibson, Owen. "A Doctor Whose Time Has Come." *The Guardian*, 10 March 2005. Belam.

Haining, Peter. *Doctor Who: A Celebration; Two Decades Through Time and Space*. USA: Carol Pub Group, 1983.

Hambly, Barbara. "Regeneration – Shaping the Road Ahead." Thomas and O'Shea.

Hoskin, Dave. "The New Man: The Regeneration Of Doctor Who." *Metro* 169 (2011): 130. MasterFILE Complete.

"An Interview with Gareth Roberts." *BBC* 17 September 2011. http://www.bbc.co.uk/mobile/tv/doctorwho/news/news_17092011/index.shtml.

Kistler, Alan. *Doctor Who*: A History. UK: Lyons Press, 2013.

Layton, David. *The Humanism of Doctor Who*. Jefferson, NC:

McFarland, 2012.

Lotz, Sarah. "For the Love of Tom." Stanish and Myles.

Martin, Daniel. "Doctor Who: The Five Best and Worst Companions" *The Guardian* 28 Mar 2007. http://www.theguardian.com/culture/tvandradioblog/2 007/mar/28/doctorwhothefivebestandw

Mead, Laura. "David Tennant's Bum" Stanish and Myles.

"Moffat Talks Valeyard, River's Future & Closure." *io9* 27 July 2013. http://www.doctorwhotv.co.uk/moffat-talks-valeyard-rivers-future-closure-52047.htm

Muir, John Kenneth. *A Critical History of Doctor Who on Television.* Jefferson: NC: McFarland, 1999.

Newman, Kim. *Doctor Who.* UK: British Film Institute, 2005.

Nussbaum, Emily. "Fantastic Voyage." *New Yorker* 88.16 (2012): 126-127. *Academic Search Complete.*

"Open All Hours." *Doctor Who Confidential. Doctor Who: The Complete Sixth Series.*

Pool, Hannah. "Freema Agyeman: Question Time." *The Guardian,* 29 March 2007. Belam.

Radish, Christina. "Steven Moffat Talks *Doctor Who*, His Favorite Upcoming Episodes, Writing the Doctor and Sherlock Holmes, the 50th Anniversary, and More" *Collider* 2013. http://collider.com/steven-moffat-doctor-who-season-7-interview.

Rose, Lloyd. "What's a Girl to Do" Thomas and O'Shea 46-50.

Roth, Dan. "Moffat Reveals his Plans (and Fears) if Eccleston had Returned for Who's 50th." *Blastr* 16 Dec 2013. http://www.blastr.com/2013-12-16/moffat-reveals-his-plans-and-fears-if-eccleston-had-returned-whos-50th

Roth "Why Moffat Was Against Bringing Back Ice Warriors for New Who." *Blastr* 21 Feb 2013. http://www.blastr.com/2013-2-21/why-moffat-was-against-bringing-back-ice-warriors-new-who

Sladen, Elisabeth. *Elisabeth Sladen: The Autobiography.* UK: Aurum Press Ltd, 2011.

Stanish, Deborah and L.M. Myles. Eds. *Chicks Unravel Time: Women Journey Through Every Season of Doctor Who.* Mad Norwegian Press. Kindle Edition.

Stoker, Courtney "Maids and Masters: The Distribution of Power in Doctor Who Series Three" Stanish and Myles.

Thomas, Lynne M. and Tara O'Shea. *Chicks Dig Time Lords.* Illinois, Mad Norwegian Press, 2010.

Tulloch, John and Manuel Alvarado. *Doctor Who: The Unfolding Text.* New York: Saint Martins, 1983.

Index

214

215

217

About the Author

Valerie Estelle Frankel has won a Dream Realm Award, an Indie Excellence Award, and a *USA Book News* National Best Book Award for her *Henry Potty* parodies. She's the author of many books on pop culture, including *From Girl to Goddess: The Heroine's Journey in Myth and Legend, Buffy and the Heroine's Journey, Winning the Game of Thrones: The Host of Characters and their Agendas, Katniss the Cattail: An Unauthorized Guide to Names and Symbols in The Hunger Games, An Unexpected Parody, Teaching with Harry Potter, Harry Potter: Still Recruiting,* and *Doctor Who and the Hero's Journey.* Once a lecturer at San Jose State University, she's a frequent speaker on fantasy, myth, and pop culture. Come explore her latest research at VEFrankel.com.

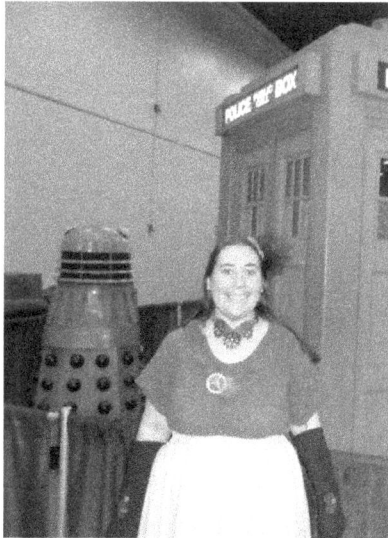

www.ingramcontent.com/pod-product-compliance
Lightning Source LLC
Chambersburg PA
CBHW031511040426
42445CB00009B/173